THE NEW GREEN REPUBLIC

THE NEW GREEN REPUBLIC

ROY MORRISON

Waterside Productions

Printed in the United States of America

First Printing, 2021

ISBN-13: 978-1-951805-88-3 print edition
ISBN-13: 978-1-951805-89-0 ebook edition

Waterside Productions
2055 Oxford Ave
Cardiff, CA 92007
www.waterside.com

TABLE OF CONTENTS

Acknowledgements

This book, of course, was shaped by the work of many. I attempt to stand on the shoulders of giants. I decided to take the Platonic dialogue form to make the questions addressed in *The New Green Republic* more accessible than usual social theory and reflect the issues of our days. In *The Republic*, Plato boldly engaged the questions of political economy, justice, and the nature of the city-state.

The New Green Republic wrestles with many of the same questions 2,450 years later addressing the nature of a prosperous and just social order. But the weight of the questions has changed. Accelerating global ecological crisis have made decisions in the twenty-first century of epochal significance, not only for humanity, but for the future of the ecosphere and all its beings.

The questions of freedom and community, of balancing rights and responsibilities, of crafting a just and healthy political order are shaped by the intertwined nature of political, economic, and social conduct. Emerson wrote:

> Web to weave, and corn to grind;
> Things are in the saddle,
> And ride mankind.

In what direction are we riding? Toward or away from self-destruction? *The New Green Republic* explores the practice of global ecological economic growth in the context of social and ecological justice. Can economy become a force for transformation and liberation? *The New Green Republic* examines markets using the price system to send clear signals for ecological conduct and help guide the path toward an ecological civilization. Ecological economic growth including ways to value and monetize ecological value through Sustainability Credits (SCs) based on the value of carbon dioxide displacement by renewable energy. I attempt to open new doors.

In writing *The New Green Republic*, I received generous help and useful critique from many. Among those who helped include Michael Swack of the Carsey School of Public Policy at UNH, who with economists Michael Tansey and Charles Tansey, Senior Fellow of the Carsey Center for Impact Finance, helped shape and inform Sustainability Credits; meteorologist and physicist Sam Miller of Plymouth State University who provided a scientist's clear view of the ecological crisis and careful review and suggestions; visionary mechanical engineers Pentti Aalto and Roger Faulkner; Luanne Baker for her encouragement and critical reading; Herman Greene of the Center for Ecozoic Studies; Bob Irving, ecological home builder; my business partner Robert Naser of R&R Renewables; and the associates Matt Coleman, Micah Brill, Andy Vecellio, Kevin O'Grady, and Jake Marley who contributed greatly to my understanding of solar energy and the renewable energy business, as well as many others who have contributed to this work. The errors to be found are mine.

INTRODUCTION AND
AUTHOR'S NOTE

The New Green Republic is written with the express understanding
that it is both within our power, and a central task for humanity
in the twenty-first century, to take the steps to build an ecological civilization. If we do not, the consequences of pollution and ecological
damage will unleash destructive geophysical forces unfolding from
bad to worse that will likely persist for thousands of generations.

The New Green Republic examines crucial political, economic,
technical, and philosophical dynamics of an ecological civilization—a civilization we must build as we travel from industrial business as usual to a sustainable prosperity.

In the broad scope of historical and social change, *The New
Green Republic* is an examination of a necessary response to the self-
destructive excesses of industrial civilization. It presents the development of a global ecological civilization as a healing response on
a global scale for the successful pursuit of ecological ends.

In the same fashion that the Enlightenment helped overcome
the power of church and aristocracy and ushered in a political and
industrial revolution, an ecological turn in the twenty-first century represent a response to the self-destructive consequences of
industrialism.

Facing gathering ecological catastrophe, there is a strange lack
of serious discussion about what can be done to transform the self-
destructive nature of business and pollution as usual. Of course,
the Republican party still remains, as I write, in the grasp of the

fossil fuel industry, and ruled by an ideology that denies reality. This is a crucial concern, but not the central global problem.

In 2020, the Republican Party is now embracing Q-anon conspiracy lunacy. But even for what still passes as sober and sane judgement, most pollution, depletion, and ecological damage is regulated by governments across the political spectrum, permitted, and legal. The billionaires and their retainers, the technocrats, the politicians, the investment bankers, are only beginning to be troubled by the path toward self-destruction they have embarked upon.

This is a system of organized self-destruction and self-delusion. The sense of collective helplessness even among the billionaires to change the course of events is similar to the remarks of the number two man in the Czech communist party and government as collapse accelerated. Even he, the most powerful and privileged member of the nomenklatura, the New Class, felt powerless to materially change the course of events one iota.

A social system is not an ecosystem. Our self-destructive social system is, in fact, consciously and unconsciously ignoring and transgressing the material realities that govern ecosystems local and global as we are suffering the ever-worsening ecological consequences from fire tornadoes, monster storms, killer droughts, and killer floods. And worse is surely yet to come.

In some ways, our times are metaphorically similar to 1774 or 1775 in the colonies—a time of imperial business as usual, but also not of just grumbling, but organizing. In 1776, led to the shot heard around the world fired by embattled farmer militia in Concord, Massachusetts at a bridge crossing the Concord River. Today, I can walk into a pleasant Minuteman Park bordered by the same old houses and memorials to fallen Minutemen and slain Red Coats.

It's good to remember that we live in similar times redolent with necessity and possibility for dramatic social change where excess will bring forth countervailing and healing responses.

In 2020, the murder of George Floyd made Black Lives Matter and the words No Justice No Peace, in the midst of a global pandemic, a common call to action for millions and millions recognizing the necessity for systemic change. We live in a time when we must fight for ecological and social justice. That is our inescapable reality.

We have built a global industrial system in which: maximizing profits = maximizing externalities = maximizing pollution. Externalities mean pollution for free and shifting costs to those downwind or to future generations. To continue this behavior by market and nonmarket systems is a recipe for disaster and collapse. This is not a right wing or left wing standpoint.

The voluntary international pledges by the world's nations made in Paris in 2015 to reduce greenhouse gas emissions—in order to keep a rise in average global temperatures below 2 degrees Celsius—were welcome. But they are unlikely to be adequate to even reach a goal that would permit a dangerous, but allegedly manageable, increase in global temperature. Physics will overcome wishful thinking and self-delusion. It's time to ask serious questions and take action.

The New Green Republic was written to engage the questions of serious alternatives to business as usual within the context of political democracy and an ecological market where economic growth means ecological improvement and the regeneration of natural capital. In an ecological civilization: maximizing profits = regeneration of natural capital = minimizing externalities.

For some, these are heretical statements. The human project, the Anthropocene, has been judged and convicted of irredeemable crimes against the biosphere. A future for civilization, if we are to have one, for some is to be found in de-growth and a radical contraction of economic activity globally. I take another view of human prospect and possibility.

The New Green Republic explores the shape of a future ecological civilization. This is a social order where economic growth means ecological improvement and the regeneration of natural capital. Ecological economic growth rests on the pursuit of sustainability aimed at a global convergence on sustainability and prosperity for all. It means trillions of dollars in investments in a sustainable future.

The New Green Republic considers the nature and basis of such a system where the pursuit of social and ecological justice is integral to its success, and where fiduciary responsibility means both the regeneration of natural capital and the growth of finance capital.

The New Green Republic recognizes that sustainability as self-conscious human intention is now integral to the fundamental coevolutionary dynamic of sustainability. Sustainability in action means life in response to all influences evolves to help maintain the biosphere as maximally suitable for all life. This is a virtuous circle of coevolutionary call and response. As the ecosphere changes, life changes, the ecosphere changes, and on and on.

Human self-consciousness and social behavior are now part of this basic dynamic of the biosphere that has enabled life to survive periodic mass extinction and once again thrive. Sustainability as conscious human social behavior has become one expression of the dynamic of process ecology in motion where the behavior of an ecosystem as a whole has profound consequences.

By addressing an ecological civilization, *The New Green Republic* is concerned with more than the fate of a single ecological nation or city-state somehow surviving as a sustainable island in a polluted and afflicted sea.

In the twenty-first century, ultimately, we will sink or float together. *The New Green Republic* is concerned with more than the evolution of single states or nations. It offers prescriptions for a path toward the globalization of a sustainable ecological order. These ecological ends become social action in support of a restored and sustainable global ecosystem.

The New Green Republic is a call for diverse healing responses to industrial excess, not for a unitary world state. As Kant wisely pointed out in *Perpetual Peace*, "... the amalgamation of states under one superior power ... would end in one universal monarchy, and laws always lose in vigor what government gains in extent, hence a soulless despotism falls into anarchy after stifling the seeds of the good."

Nor is the relevance of *The New Green Republic* limited to a world of liberal multiparty democracies. *The New Green Republic* is a recipe for a global convergence on a prosperous sustainable ecological civilization that rests on three key pillars supporting a durable and successful global ecological transformation.

First, sustainable global economic growth that means the regeneration of natural capital along with the growth of finance capital. Second, the pursuit of social and ecological justice must include global mechanisms for the transfer of technology and capital from rich to poor for productive investment in the efficient renewable energy and the sustainability infrastructure. Third, the continued and successful transformation of a global war system to a peace system that is very much supported by the global pursuit of social and ecological justice and a global ecological growth strategy.

These three principles—a global ecological growth agenda, pursuit of social and ecological justice, and peace—can be applicable to a wide range of nations, including those organized on hierarchical or theocratic principles that embrace the pursuit of the ecological imperative. For an ecological civilization, ecological justice is not simply an expression of a liberal concept of justice as fairness, or of natural rights understood through reason. Social and ecological justice is integral to an ecological future, and therefore is rooted in the pursuit of self-interest and community interest for all.

The New Green Republic includes examination of a number of carrots and sticks to encourage and reward the common global pursuit of an ecological agenda to be wielded by all states, democratic or not, that have embraced the pursuit of an ecological civilization.

China, for example, has made building an ecological civilization a basis for state policy and is now global leader in solar and wind production as well as reforestation, and is on a path to cap and reduce carbon dioxide emissions. This is absolutely crucial if we are to keep global temperature increases below 2 degrees centigrade. Many of the themes and mechanisms discussed in *The New Green Republic* are relevant to China, whether or not the Chinese choose to embrace its political prescriptions. China, as the world's second-largest economy and global factory, must continue to pursue an ecological path.

History did not end with the collapse of the Berlin Wall. We are faced with a choice between a prosperous and sustainable ecological future, or ecological and civilizational collapse if we do not embrace an ecological path.

The good news is that prospects for ecological economic growth open up new creative venues for ecological value and sustainability and monetizing such values.

Ecological economic growth (EEG) is the means to make economic growth result in ecological improvement, not further destruction. EEG recognizes the fundamental difference that a global market system must make between the pursuit of profit that results in ecological improvement and an increase in social and ecological justice and profit that means ecological destruction and impoverishment for the many.

A global renewable energy transformation to replace all fossil fuels and nuclear energy is a paradigmatic example of economic growth leading to ecological improvement, and one that must be pursued in the context of the pursuit of social and ecological justice.

The New Green Republic will consider new ways of both valuing and monetizing sustainability for its essential worth and prod for ecological economic growth and ecological improvement. Sustainability Credits (SCs) will be created by the displacement by renewables of one metric ton of carbon dioxide emissions valued by the National Academy of Sciences at one hundred dollars. SCs will be monetized on the books of a Green Bank or Bank of the Commons as paid in capital and as cash. We will see how SCs can generate the fifty trillion dollars estimated by JPMorgan Chase needed to finance investment in global renewable energy transformation from 2020 to 2050.

The New Green Republic is more than airy-fairy good wishes. It's about more than wishing corporate capitalism to go away. *The New Green Republic* presents a venue for social change and sustainable economic growth and social and ecological justice. A desirable, and, I hope, inspiring path forward.

History and future prospects did not end with the triumph of liberal corporate capitalism over Soviet communism. The challenge of the twenty-first century and beyond is building a global ecological civilization in all its glory from industrial business as usual. A Green Republic is a venue for such a grand transformation. The book is intended to inspire discussion and action.

DRAMATIS PERSONAE
(IN ORDER APPEARING)

Sam Morrison...... conservation biologist and theorist

Bob Irving........... carpenter, gardener, and sustainable home building contractor

Pentti Aalto......... mechanical engineer, expert in energy systems and energy markets

Ruth Johnson....... psychiatric clinician and brain scholar

Phil Clark............. physicist and professor of earth sciences

Wang Li............... ecologist and scholar

Meagan Simons... conservation biologist and philosopher

The participants are inspired by real people of long acquaintance, some with real names, but they are all used fictitiously as avatars representing arguments and ideas. As avatars for ideas, I mean no offense to the real people who, of course, are not responsible for this work or its opinions or ideas. Any errors or mistakes are entirely my own. It felt right to me, as Plato did, to have the names of real people represent participants in his dialogues.

1. First Problems

Sam Morrison: We have a problem.

Bob Irving: We haven't started and we already have a problem?

Pentti Aalto: Of course, we have many problems. Let me tell you. As I see it...

Ruth Johnson: Yes, a problem of unwrapping the bundle of first things. Where are we? What are we? What do we know? Where are we going?

Pentti Aalto: Not exactly what I was thinking—it's the problem of politics and polity, a problem of finding and keeping the balance between freedom and community, the problem of economics and technology, the problem of sustainability and the relationship between ecosphere and social sphere, how to make economic growth mean ecological improvement while also pursuing social and ecological justice...

Wang Li: And how to make the price system send clear signals for sustainability in markets and nonmarkets, and how to make the creation and preservation of ecological value, for example, from displacement of carbon dioxide emissions an asset accounted for balance sheets that helps properly guide and reward economic behavior.

Bob Irving: That seems so far from the business realities that I wrestle with every day.

Sam Morrison: All that's true. But I was just thinking about getting some coffee and Danish, or scones as you desire. Something to start.

Pentti Aalto: From Zabar's?

Sam Morrison: Of course. Where else?

Bob Irving: That's the kind of problem I can solve, I'll put the order in.

Phil Clark: A blessed choice.

Wang Li: Decaf for me. And rugelach.

Bob Irving: Pots of caf and decaf. Danish, rugelach, scones if they have them.

Wang Li: Problem solved.

Pentti Aalto: That was easier than we thought.

Phil Clark: At least for takeout.

Sam Morrison: OK. Now to put my toe gingerly, oh-so-gingerly, into the deep, fast-running waters.

Ruth Johnson: Brave man.

Wang Li: Or foolish.

Ruth Johnson: That's a decision for posterity.

Wang Li: It's like when Chou En Lai was asked about what he thought about the consequence of the French Revolution. It's said he replied, "Too early to say."

Pentti Aalto: We certainly can't know in the midst of it. We can have opinions, the value and meaning is irreducibly tied into the work itself.

Phil Clark: Wittgenstein?

Pentti Aalto: Sort of. He said it much more elegantly.

Sam Morrison: In any case, sticking my toe into the river of choice and chance and change, we have been asked to outline for the New Continental Congress the broad parameters of a Constitutional order, a guiding document for a viable and sustainable Green Republic for the Western Hemispheric Union, and perhaps beyond.

Wang Li: What that means, of course, is essentially vague. It could be a new Ten Commandments, or two-thousand commandments for that matter.

Pentti Aalto: A postal manual for an ecological civilization. I don't think so. Instead, we need mechanisms—mechanisms that help ecological markets and politics make sense.

Ruth Johnson: I don't think so either. We face a philosophical and political undertaking. For it to be worth completing, it must have a spiritual and political resonance. It must be a document that moves people to action, that guides their action, and works as circumstances change and we face situations that will suddenly emerge that do not exist now.

Sam Morrison: Yes, that's the task. What is a Green Republic? What does it mean? How does it work? How does it endure?

Ruth Johnson: Notice that the task is for a Green Republic, not just for an ecological civilization of any sort. I have my opinion. Social possibilities and social imagination are not limited by the shape of a Green Republic. We're here to discuss the shape of a Green Republic, not to impose it or export it. Yes, we are, and I believe this for good reasons. But, also recognizing that while we believe the Green Republic is the way, it is not necessarily the only way. I think it's the best answer and most appealing to me in terms of resolving the underlying social dynamic of the tensions between freedom and community. But it's not the only choice. Nor is the existence of a Green Republic in name only mean that it will continue to behave in an ecological fashion.

Wang Li: Yes. China has chosen and it actively pursues an ecological civilization to guide and condition sustainable growth within the context of political organization guided by the Communist Party of China.

Sam Morrison: The East may be green. And by necessity, it may converge on many of the same kind of mechanisms guiding economy, society, and technology that we are looking at, but it is not following the path of a Green Republic.

Phil Clark: For better or for worse.

Wang Li: This discussion is not attempting to explore if there is only one way, or even the best way, for the operation and maintenance of an ecological civilization to achieve an enduring, prosperous, and sustainable civilization.

Bob Irving: We keep talking about an ecological civilization. Exactly, or more or less, what the hell is that? *Happy Days*. The Red Sox always win, and Homer Simpson is now smart?

Pentti Aalto: I'll give it a go. An ecological civilization may be defined simply in practice by two basic attributes. First, that economic activity and growth leads to ecological improvement and the restoration of the living world—that can be inelegantly labeled as natural capital. Second, that economic growth is conditioned by the pursuit not only of sustainability, but social and ecological justice, which are essential in the long run for maintaining social and ecological health. In principle, this is not limited to market economies or liberal democracies.

Sam Morrison: There's almost certainly not just one way toward a sustainable future. Our task is to explore the elements a Green Republic, not to determine the potential for authoritarian and theocratic systems to reach ecological ends, if that's what they pursue.

Pentti Aalto: The supposition that brings us together, or the conceit as you would have it, is that a Green Republic with a strong and participatory democracy has advantages in pursuing and maintaining the balance between freedom and community, between expansion and limitation conditioned by ecological consequences and social and ecological justice, enabling it in the long run to follow an ecological path ultimately on the basis of one person, one vote.

Phil Clark: But we are not writing a General Theory of Ecological Transformation. We assume, bravely or foolishly, that democracy is the stick that stirs the sustainability drink, despite the existing democratically permitted conduct of the leading industrial polluters. Or maybe we are just asserting or hoping, despite evidence to the contrary, democracy could.

Pentti Aalto: Our Green Republic on a scale of several hundred million people will not be a unitary hierarchy with a single representative body. Its nature, in my view, will reflect a great multiplicity of self-managing and democratic governed groups guided by the principle of subsidiarity where decisions are made with deference to those most directly affected.

Ruth Johnson: A sort of home rule as we have in NH decided by open-to-all town meetings. For example, the Green Republic mandates the practice of a sustainable forestry and agriculture, including the sequestration of carbon dioxide. How this is done is up to local decisions within broad boundaries and in accord with local ecological development plans.

Phil Clark: Meaning they would not be permitted to cut down all the trees and end the forest problem forever?

Bob Irving: Is that a scientist's prudent data-driven skepticism or cynical realism?

Phil Clark: Good question. Some of both, I suppose. I'm just not ready to drink the Kool-Aid. Important errors are sometimes made in the unexamined acceptance of assumptions that everyone "knows" are true. An axiom is an axiom, not data or truth driven. Everything may be questioned, examined, and reexamined.

Sam Morrison: It's the actions of a Green Republic based on the principles we articulate that we are considering. We'll be getting into the dynamics of the ecological transformation that suggest to me the advantages possessed by strong democratic social orders in crafting and maintaining a healing response to industrial excess and the creation of effective new levels of organization and complexity to move away from the self-destructive proclivities of industrial business and pollution as usual. That said, I don't want to and, more to the point, we can't just slam the door on others following a different path.

Bob Irving: Wait. You're claiming the saving grace of a Green Republic—that we have hardly begun to discuss—is that it makes things more complicated. Aren't our lives complicated enough already? Isn't this about small is beautiful and back to the land away from factory farms?

Ruth Johnson: A practical example is of a giant city with all buildings identical square boxes laid out in a grid with uniform identical park spaces between them providing the joy of Stalinist architecture or some of enormous housing projects. Compare this to a city of diverse neighborhoods, each with their own character and diverse activities, their own often unique architectural features and layouts, and local and ever-evolving specialties and interests old and new, each developing their own pattern language that has facilitated development of the local character.

Sam Morrison: The good news is there's both history and science supporting the idea that increasing complexity can be useful and beneficial for the system as a whole. Beneficial complexity is an expression of feedback, call and response, information and knowledge, learning in motion. The five-dollar word is cybernetics. But the plain message is that more knowledge and more communication lead to a useful increase in complexity, living texture, many life ways expressed and vital becoming collectively one.

Sam Morrison: This is where—getting philosophical—the split between ontology and epistemology begins to disappear. The received wisdom from Plato onward manifests in our confidence in a world of abstract categories and clear separation and our propensity to cut things to pieces, begins to make less and less sense in the face of living reality. Like the sudden discovery that the roots of forest trees are connected by a matt of mycelium that can extend for thousands of miles. Where does the single individual end?

Phil Clark: That makes sense to me as a data man that defining arbitrary categories is just that, arbitrary, and should be considered with some sense of skepticism that can and will lead to a more useful reshuffling of categories. This should remind us that categories that seem real to us are just that, to a substantial degree, our invention.

Ruth Johnson: Borges wrote a wonderful story about his fanciful universal encyclopedia with magical categories.

Sam Morrison: Well said. The tension between unity and diversity has deep social and biological meaning. We now understand, for instance, that the weeping willows in the forest are all genetic clones reproducing from twigs broken off and somehow taking root. The fact that we become conscious of patterns, integration and their meanings is the power of gestalt psychology. It has clear evolutionary survival value in helping see the lion hiding near the water hole that also challenges our propensity to name and categorize and separate.

Ruth Johnson: But on the downside it also explains the power of racist tropes. In any case, we are rooted in a world of wondrous complexity and interconnection. But to be clear, we are talking about the core of building an ecological civilization is the social power to create new forms expressing sustainability in response to the self-destructive conduct of industrial civilization. This is the emergent power of new forms and increasing complexity that can mean fundamental and healing social change of an ecological civilization. We are not limited by historic nostrums defining the limits of possibility.

Pentti Aalto: This is quite the opposite of a future featureless Absolute mocked by Hegel as "the night in which all cows are black." What the prospect of global ecological social change implies, at its center, is continuous social recreation and a myriad of themes and variation. We cannot be describing a static and predictable future, or end of history nonsense with the creation of an ecological civilization, any more than Francis Fukuyama accurately predicted the end of history with the triumph of liberal capitalist democracy over Soviet communism. History has shown this was no more than a fleeting moment, or a squandered opportunity.

Bob Irving: That I understand. A friend told me that "at night, all cows are black" is a Yiddish proverb meaning in the dark, all women look the same. It was a deliberately nasty comment used by Hegel in the early nineteenth century high class intellectual debates over Absolutes.

Ruth Johnson: Yes, on the one hand we have future limitless possibility to be manifest by an ecological future. On the other hand, we must recognize that rapid change is often dislocating and unpleasant for many. On a system scale, increasing complexity and building more relationships and larger networks reduces entropy and provides feedback that increases stability. If we look at society with global interconnections, its behavior will reflect the actions of the whole as more than the sum of its parts as a global ecosystem. And the behavior that the Green Republic is about is the pursuit of sustainability with all its attendant social changes.

Pentti Aalto: In the long run, human society evolved and increased the level of size, sophistication, and scale from bands, to clans, to tribes, to kings, and on and on, driven by a need to resolve new and emerging problems presented by growth and new scales. No one said, yeah let's go from a band of twenty to a nation of one billion or a global ecological civilization of seven to nine billion.

Ruth Johnson: This does not mean in a networked global civilization of nine billion that the optimal organizational size might not still be between two hundred and six hundred people. This is about the limit for ongoing intimate relations for all members. Thirty million small organizations of three hundred people as interdependent business and social institutions and intimate cohorts might emerge as opposed to thirty thousand large organizations of one hundred thousand people. Three hundred to six hundred might be the right size that limits bureaucracy and encourages self-management and personal relationships among all the participants. Decentralization, confederation, and cooperation may enormously increase both the volume of communication and the number of entities and reduce their size on the base micro-scale avoiding industrialism's dis-economies of scale in a computer mediated information age.

Phil Clark: Like the many small cooperatives and firms in Emilia-Romano region in Italy forming ever-shifting alliances and partnerships on projects and being competitive and effective on the world scale. The plan here is to unleash this diverse multitude in the pursuit of ecological ends. This is constructivist intent on a high order like the self-reinforcing components of a complex ecosystem forming ever-shifting interactions that both cooperate and compete with other components.

Bob Irving: OK. I get it. The intent may be bigger and grander. Global in intent, composed of many more participating entities organized and self-organized in many fashions.

Sam Morrison: These diverse organizational forms imply the exercise of both individual and collective social power. On the freedom and community continuum, the individual has substantial degrees of freedom, but that freedom is nested and protected within the local organizations, businesses, schools, housing, and health systems that they belong to and take part in. Thus, freedom and community are mutually self-enforcing for the benefit of both individual and community. The individual has freedom and inalienable rights. But these rights are within the responsibility that must be assumed by individuals and are expressed by the community. The free individual acts and lives within the structures, protection, and strictures chosen democratically by the community. The model is much closer to that of associative democracy, the world of membership and voting in diverse organizations that constitute of our social lives as opposed to the view of an individual clothed in constitutional rights alone as one person in a sea of hundreds of millions or billions of other individuals. The goal is for each person to have real democratic power of one person, one vote in all social organizations in which she participates.

Bob Irving: Yeah, life as a near limitless number of condo association meetings.

Pentti Aalto: I think the truth is that as Churchill said, democracy is the worst form of government, except for all the others.

Ruth Johnson: It's important to remember the virtues of democracy, as messy as it may be. The alternatives to voting and democracy are at one pole authoritarianism of many kinds, and the other consensus seeking which means group decisions where everyone has their say and is satisfied. This does not mean unanimity, but acceptance of group consensus. Rousseau, for one, was attracted by concepts of a naturally arising "General Will" in a state that "needs very few laws; and in so far as it becomes necessary to promulgate new ones, this necessity is universally recognized." This unfortunately is an easy formula for the rise of dictatorial rule and a failure to address naturally arising conflicting interests along lines of class, location, age, ethnicity, et cetera. A Green Republic is about more democratic venues, not fewer.

2. Freedom & Community?

R uth Johnson: This raises for me the question what is freedom?
Bob Irving: To do what I want, when I want?

Ruth Johnson: But the problem that Isaiah Berlin famously put his finger on in "Two Concepts of Liberty" is, of course, your right to swing your fist ends when you reach my nose. Negative liberty is the right to be free of the unjust imposition of outside power. "If I am prevented by others from doing what I could otherwise do, I am to that degree unfree..." The challenge for a Green Republic is that it posits very much the interaction between freedom and community as essential for the practice of positive liberty, and protection from the imposition of outside power, so-called negative liberty. What's very much overlooked in the depth of Berlin's analysis are questions of justice he attached to the freedom of the rich. "Everything is what it is: liberty is liberty, not equality or fairness or justice or culture, or human happiness or a quiet conscience. If the liberty of myself or my class or nation depends on the misery of a number of other human beings, the system which promotes this is unjust and immoral."

Wang Li: Rousseau expressed similar sentiments, but with more cynicism. In *The Social Contract*, he wrote, "The Strongest man is never strong enough to be always master, unless he transforms his power into right, and obedience into duty."

Sam Morrison: The suggestion for the Green Republic is that the choice is not between an overarching state to enforce the rules and regs or anarchist freedom from all constraint, but rather there are strong democratic community-based membership structures

11

that also make clear individual responsibilities and rights manifest, protected, and establish a dynamic balance between rights and responsibilities. The common error of both libertarians and the rich is to ignore the essential nature of negative liberties, for others to be free from pollution and exploitation, and the consequences of their conduct as polluters and oppressors acting in pursuit of their freedom.

Ruth Johnson: Community in this case is the X factor interposed between individual and government that both protects and conditions freedom. That's the place where rights and responsibilities and the balance between the two are manifest.

Sam Morrison: Both freedom and community are individual and social artifacts. The Mondragon cooperatives in the Basque region of Spain have built this kind of interlocking set of democratic membership co-ops that are resolutely self-managing, entrepreneurial, based on one person, one vote. At the same time, Basque culture is conservative, wary of individual efforts outside of the group where freedom is quite explicitly understood as being interconnected with community.

Ruth Johnson: So there are not limitations on non-joiners to these collective groups in the interest of freedom for individuals.

Sam Morrison: There are strong social and economic incentives to take advantage of the many cooperative institutions through membership. But the Mondragon co-ops have realized that you cannot and should not mandate cooperation. It can be offered but not imposed.

Ruth Johnson: That's the deciding line between a healthy regard for both freedom and community and quite the opposite.

Bob Irving: Hence mandatory participation in an endless series of condo-association style meetings is not required.

3. Sustainability Rising

Pentti Aalto: It's an empirical truth that numerous human civilizations have behaved sustainably. Those were not high technology industrial civilizations. But it's also clear today that places like Denmark and Iceland have shown that sustainability is possible now. But islands of the sustainable cannot flourish amidst global ecological chaos.

Bob Irving: Sustainability is an expression of ecosystems that are nested together from local to global, from backyard ponds to oceans, and of effective human choices from neighborhood to planet. Fit together and supporting one another like a timber frame.

Sam Morrison: Sustainability is ultimately an emergent social phenomenon, humanity's conscious participation in the fundamental biological processes of sustainability, of life's response to all influences in ways that are maximally favorable for all life.

Wang Li: Sustainability is coevolution in action between life and the ecosphere. Life changes in response to changes in the ecosphere, and the ecosphere changes in response to life. This is really extraordinary, how life has shaped the planet as the planet has shaped life. Life has created and maintains the oxygen atmosphere and has responded to periodic mass extinctions in a manner that will allow life to reshape the ecosphere and once again thrive.

Sam Morrison: And now sustainability has become a conscious human behavior acting in support of ecological survival.

Phil Clark: Yes, what this means in the most fundamental way is that at bottom, the issue is social not technical.

Pentti Aalto: Are you sure?

Phil Clark: Not ultimately technical. There are technical challenges. But certainly nothing insurmountable given that what's at stake is the choice between global collapse of civilization or sustainable prosperity. Excess leads to countervailing and healing response both biologically and socially. What's emerging here is a Green Republic. Something new under the sun whose time apparently has come. Something new, more than the sum of its parts. Solid matter emerging from quantum chaos if we have enough atoms.

Wang Li: And yet, until recently, we have largely been unwilling to pursue any kind of effective program that would realistically solve the problem. This is not just a matter of politics, but of will and intention. "Voluntary" national commitments for greenhouse gas reduction does not begin to prevent global warming from exceeding the 2 degree centigrade level that is the supposed point inviting unmanageable catastrophic changes.

Phil Clark: Yes, the political and social power of the polluters and business as usual had prevented even a serious discussion of what needs to be done. The economic arguments of polluters and their political power maintained their ability to continue not only their ability to poison for free, but to be subsidized directly and indirectly while doing so.

Bob Irving: We were pouring gasoline on the fire. Doing little to make serious changes to stop the march toward ecological catastrophe.

Pentti Aalto: There was no clear right wing or left wing or centrist plan of competing programs for sustainability. It wasn't a right wing or left wing dispute. Pollution was in the saddle and rode humanity.

Sam Morrison: It is only the gravity of the situation that's led to the irresistible mandate for a Green Republic in response to the clear and present danger of ecological catastrophe. But the context is the pursuit of sustainability and ecological and social justice as essential concomitants for the successful pursuit of sustainability. And social and ecological justice for all raises all kinds of issues that must be attended to given existing enormous disparities of wealth and of power.

Wang Li: That leads to both the necessity and the promise of global ecological economic growth through the productive investment globally of trillions for renewable energy and ecological transformation to build globally a much larger economy fairly distributed while dramatically reducing pollution, depletion, and ecological damage.

Bob Irving: And we are moved to act by the need to take concerted action while there is still a credible option to save ourselves and the ecosphere from tragedy.

Phil Clark: Yes, but I'm not sure if it's really socially and politically possible for us to make the choices. That's the elephant in the room that was apparently not polite to recognize despite its massive and smelly presence.

Bob Irving: Yes, it was too easy to say it was a difficult technical problem. Couldn't do it. Too expensive. Nothing can be done. Shut your eyes. Stepping back as a carpenter, much of this is about what you count and how you count it.

Sam Morrison: We are really good at counting the last cent of destructive profits, but not at all good at accounting for the value of ecological sustainability, of repairing ecosystems, eliminating pollution, reversing depletion, or ending ecological damage. Much of a Green Republic is deciding on what is counted and how; what is monetized and how. The economist would say eliminate externalities. Hillel would say treat others as you would want to be treated. In this sense, eliminating externalities would be a moral statement clothed in market rules. That's the subtext of the pursuit of sustainability that encompasses the economic, biological, and social.

Pentti Aalto: That definition does not make the spirit soar. But at some point, even an academy and congress of fools can't avoid the obvious. Now cognizant, at last, that the challenge is political and social, and the technical a matter of method and implementation, the biggest challenge is for us to make the fundamental choices to pursue sustainability.

Sam Morrison: Hence the Green Republic. Implicit is that there is no Hobbesian Leviathan or wise philosopher kings running the show. It's not about a world of obedient subjects and all-knowing administrative state. Green Republic is closer to a twenty-first century version of the popular nineteenth century injunction that the government is best that governs least, now meaning government on an appropriately limited scale in the context of the Green Republic embracing participation, self-management, self-organization, community power, and information age robust privacy protection manifest in personal space as well as in cyberspace and democracy far beyond a quadrennial vote for president. Community and community institutions are an essential counter balance to government power.

Pentti Aalto: More self-management. More democratic organization and participation across the social and economic spheres. Not relying on orders from the Capital. Yes, there is a structure of law, regulation, ecological market rules, ecologically based taxation, sustainability's value from ecological improvement on balance sheets, legal redefinition of fiduciary responsibility that makes pursuing profit also mean the pursuit of ecological improvement within the context of social and ecological justice. The basic rules of the ecological road and the Green Republic. Government is not weak, but it is limited in the context of balancing rights and responsibilities, which is the essential role of community.

Ruth Johnson: What you are suggesting is that ultimately the Green Republic sits midway on a continuum between freedom on one end—which would be anarchism without a state—and community, and on the other end, a unitary and hierarchical social order, a theocracy, technocracy, or authoritarianism. What's interesting is that the freedom end of the continuum appeals to both some on the left and the right desiring to be free of limitations from government, which can include being free to pollute. Similarly, the community end of the continuum appeals to the inclination of the right, the theocratic and authoritarian, and the left of Stalinist, authoritarian mien.

Sam Morrison: There is, and must be, a ceaseless push-pull within a Green Republic between these two poles. The Green Republic is ever-balancing and equilibrating on all levels these two conflicting and complementary imperatives of freedom and community that inform the transformation from a self-destructive industrial social order to ecological civilization. It defers to the local in pursuit of ecological and social justice in the context of economic growth, meaning ecological improvement. And for me, that means the individual and social entrepreneurship and self-management is integral to these rights and behaviors that puts flesh on the bones on sustainability—the economic, the ecological, the social.

Wang Li: In some ways, to me this dynamic of self-management, democratic participation, and control in all sorts of community organizations from business to housing to schools and beyond, has the flavor of Murray Bookchin's libertarian municipalism. It's a structure for local empowerment, a conditional anarchist model balancing rights and responsibilities.

Sam Morrison: Yes. Within the context of the structure of a Green Republic.

Wang Li: Libertarian municipalism as anarchism metaphorically acting as the mitochondria providing crucial energy subsumed with the cells of the Green Republic. Anarchism as libertarian municipalism functioning as both a stabilizing force that plays a crucial role in both helping maintain a balance between freedom and community and as a strong force for decentralized deep democracy highly resistant to any attempts to subvert the purposes of the Green Republic from both above and below.

Bob Irving: So you recognize that the Green Republic is not and will never be a utopia function for ever and ever once established.

Wang Li: No, this is always contested terrain. That's the brief for possibility and reality.

Sam Morrison: No utopia. A deep democracy balancing freedom and community. Of course, Murray Bookchin would say that Libertarian Municipalism is both means and the end for a just and ecological future. The Green Republic would represent the state and business as usual. Libertarian Municipalism would struggle for power to supplant the state and capitalism. For Bookchin, a growth of cooperative business and other institutions represent a communitarianism that would historically exist on the margins.

Ruth Johnson: The Green Republic supposes that the laws, regulations, market rules of the Green Republic for ecological economic growth and social and ecological justice combined with strong local democracy and economic justice establishes the basis for an enduring social and economic system, an ecological civilization.

Wang Li: Is this more than just social democracy in new clothes to be undermined over time by capitalist imperatives combining unlimited greed and indifference to the self-destruction from pollution, depletion, and ecological damage?

Sam Morrison: I would say that the Green Republic and ecological civilization rest upon a series of essential and necessary radical reforms. Thomas Piketty in *Capital and Ideology* wrote, "Inequality is neither economic nor technological; it is ideological and political." Piketty details a history of successful radical reforms. The radical reforms of a Green Republic are a recipe for the creation of durable social and ecological justice and for ecological survival and prosperity. And crucially, the valuation and monetization of ecological value and ecological improvement can create trillions of dollars for productive investment and ecological transformation, for fairness and justice.

Wang Li: The Green Republic addresses not merely the issues of social justice and deepening global inequality that is the focus of Piketty's work. The paramount global challenge that must be addressed is that of ecological crisis. Ecological justice must be an equal imperative to social justice.

Sam Morrison: The Green Republic is more than restoration of the elements of social democracy dismantled progressively and to greater or lesser extents by the rich and powerful in the interest of their wealth and profit at the expense of working people and the poor. That is not a new story. The Green Republic creates a structure for ecological survival and for social and ecological justice.

This structure limits the pursuit of profit, the conduct of capital to economic action that makes economic growth lead to ecological improvement in the context of social and ecological justice. This can employ various social democratic tools like living wages, basic income, national heath care, progressive ecological taxation, and more. What's new and different is the wealth creation and ecological economic growth through the monetization of ecological value through Sustainability Credits (SCs).

Pentti Aalto: The Green Republic understands three essential points. First, that the consequences of economic growth can lead to ecological improvement given proper market rules, laws, and regulations. This means in principle enormous amounts of nondestructive economic growth is possible. Second, that profit can and must be in context of social and ecological justice. Third, that the monetization of ecological value opens the path toward trillions in sustainable investment. Merely reinstituting social democratic measures in the interest of equality will likely not transform the march to ecological catastrophe.

Sam Morrison: Of course, the challenge is the great rising from below likely to be essential to establish the Green Republic and its structural elements. The existence of a Green Republic will be always under threat and abuse. Its survival is dependent on a structure of deep democracy and local empowerment that can struggle and fight to maintain the balance, the golden mean, between freedom and community of a Green Republic. But the benefits of a functioning Green Republic will be broadly expressed through sustainable ecological economic growth and a larger economy, an expanded zone of freedom and love expressed in part through a basic income grant and a global convergence on sustainable norms and social and ecological justice for all as one of the consequences of ecological global economic growth and monetization of restorative ecological conduct.

4. Manifesting First Principles
of a Green Republic

Ruth Johnson: And I say we must make these first principles for a Green Republic clear as the basis for all that follows.

Robert Irving: How the hell can we do that?

Pentti Aalto: That's what I think we are about, establishing a framework for a Green Republic. The conceit is that we are drafting a social contract that has social, political, and moral force, not so much as a legal contract, but as a common understanding and guide to future action. Talking about balancing freedom and community is not a math equation, but a moral, social, and aspirational assertion, an operating assertion.

Ruth Johnson: And that logically should come right at the beginning. In the constitutional document.

Pentti Aalto: Yes. Like Article One or the preamble. Right in your face for everyone to see.

Sam Morrison: I've been doing some drafting of language on this.

Phil Clark: Big surprise.

Wang Li: I'm shocked.

Bob Irving: Shocked.

Pentti Aalto: So …

Sam Morrison: So, I propose Article One: Ecological Conduct. I'll read it from the notes on my cell phone.

Article One: Ecological Conduct

Section One: The Rights and Responsibility to protect, sustain, and enjoy ecological well-being and health shall be a fundamental principle and duty of this Republic.

Section Two: All economic and ecologically entailed actions in this Republic shall be guided by principles under law that support the improvement and regeneration of natural capital and the advancement of social and ecological justice.

Section Three: Fiduciary responsibility under law shall be defined as the prudent management of finance capital for the improvement and restoration of natural capital, and the advancement of social and ecological justice.

Phil Clark: Interesting. What I like is the clear affirmative duty of Section One.

Bob Irving: Yes, that's clear enough. It's says from the jump a Green Republic shall be green. Why not stop there? Short and sweet.

Ruth Johnson: I see the value of Sections Two and Three in putting meat on the bones of Section One. It says we can't just pay lip service to ecological conduct and continue business, profit, and pollution as usual. And of course, you want us all to swallow for now and for the indefinite future the notion of markets, profit, economic growth, private property, rich and poor, winners and losers.

Sam Morrison: Yes. I am not suggesting this is the best of all possible worlds. Rather, I am saying that we cannot save and redeem civilization in the twenty-first century and beyond by saying, "Step one: not only abolish corporate capitalism, but markets and economic growth."

Phil Clark: Call it a realism doctrine. Making the best out of the world we have as opposed to conjuring into existence the world we want. Ecological collapse will do much to abolish capitalism and markets as we know it, but not in the way we would appreciate.

Wang Li: Again, embracing radical reform as opposed to revolution.

Sam Morrison: Yes, the supposition is that we are accommodating the pursuit of profit and greed, limited and purposed for socially useful ends.

Ying Hue: That's was Adam Smith's conceit in *The Wealth of Nations* and look where that got us. Where we are.

Sam Morrison: Smith also wrote *A Theory of Moral Sentiments*, and I think he would argue that his trust was placed too strongly on moral sentiments and politics overcoming the willingness of business people to connive and conspire, of which he was fully cognizant. Our Section One asserts the root ecological basis of the Green Republic, market or not.

Pentti Aalto: Yes. Sections Two and Three raise both the business question, and, without saying it, the engineering and implementation question, as well as the nature of the bottom line.

Phil Clark: Yes, this is a brief not only for an industrial ecology, but for ecological methods for all productive action: for farming, forestry, aquaculture, industry.

Wang Li: You can't just say in a Green Republic, "my fiduciary responsibility made me pollute and destroy." Now you have to say, "my fiduciary responsibility made me stop polluting and destroying. I had no other choice."

Bob Irving: Section Two sounds good, but what's the meaning of phrases like "restoration of natural capital" and "advancement of social and ecological justice." Do we need a definitions section, or have explicit definition in Article One?

Wang Li: Well, E. F. Schumacher coined the term "natural capital" in his wonderful book *Small Is Beautiful* in 1974.

Phil Clark: *Small Is Beautiful* was one of the founding documents for the pursuit of sustainability. Herman Daly, John Cobb, Robert Costanza, Amory and Hunter Lovins, Paul Hawken, Dennis and Donella Meadows, Kenneth Boulding, John Hicks, Georgescu-Roegen, Ilya Prigogine, Isabelle Stengers, and many others have contributed to the development of the natural capital concept and the inextricable connections between the economy and the environment.

Pentti Aalto: I like the work of the International Institute for Sustainable Development (IISD) from Environment Canada.

Bob Irving: It's interesting that natural capital is a relatively new term. Something that must have been completely obvious, but from something that we conveniently ignored in the rush toward industrialization and profits.

Sam Morrison: Yes, consequences of what we did and the impact on natural capital became "externalities." Something external to our accounting for profits and losses. Something we didn't even count.

Bob Irving: And therefore, there was nothing to separate pillage and its consequences from profit.

Sam Morrison: Indeed. And good news, by the way. A text from Meagan that she will be arriving soon from the Barro Colorado research station.

Phil Clark: Near the San Juan Mountains in Southwest Colorado?

Sam Morrison: No. Actually, a tropical island in Panama. Few thousand acres in the middle of the canal that's been a Smithsonian Research station for one hundred years. We've been working there studying orchid bees.

Phil Clark: The more I know, the more I learn that I don't know.

Sam Morrison: I didn't know about it either. Until I did. That's how many things unfold as a matter of discovery, new learning, and retrospective necessity. I learned, for instance, about the pain from bullet ant bites that feels like you've had your hand hit with a hammer. That's rated in the top three on the Schmidt insect sting pain index, competing with the tarantula hawk and the warrior wasp for king or queen of pain.

Phil Clark: Hence the need for Article One, Section Three on a new definition of fiduciary responsibility.

Wang Li: Putting together the contributions of many to the definition. Natural capital, I define as the natural world from which emanate all the goods and services that sustain life, and is the basis for human activity and well-being. Derrick Jensen calls natural capital "the land base." Natural capital is renewable or non-renewable. Ecosystems are paradigmatic expressions of renewable natural capital. Ecosystems can maintain, repair, replicate themselves, and evolve. Nonrenewable natural capital, like oil or iron, is formed over long periods of time and is passive. They may be considered as resource stocks. Jensen is extremely pessimistic that industrial civilization can avoid collapse or recover from the disaster.

Pentti Aalto: That remains to be seen. I don't like the terms "resources" or "stocks," which suggest things that are our possessions to consume or abuse at our pleasure, much as we do to ecosystems. Resource "stocks" is the same as the old notion of "junk DNA" because it wasn't immediately clear of the roles it played beyond protein synthesis.

Phil Clark: Like, I own it, it's mine, I can use it as I choose. But not under Article One.

Bob Irving: I'd rather say "husband" meaning carefully manage our resources stocks. If anyone can say "husband" with a straight face in the twenty-first century to activities that apply to both women and men.

Ruth Johnson: Indeed. We say carefully and responsibly managed.

Phil Clark: The devil is in the details. And the details here involve a combination of what we do and how we measure and account for the results and consequences of our actions.

Pentti Aalto: The details and the requisite accounting systems are emerging. The U.N. System of Environmental-Economic Accounting (SEEA) has the agreed-upon concepts, definitions, classifications, accounting rules, and tables for producing internationally comparable statistics on the environment and its connections with the economy.

Sam Morrison: And there is the necessary definition of ecosystems and ecosystem services, which is economist speak attempting to quantify and monetize benefits from the living world. The ecologically intact boreal forest of Canada, one of the world's great

stores of carbon and source of atmospheric regulation, was estimated to have an ecosystem services value of $3.7 trillion. It was cal-
culated in 1997 that the total value of seventeen ecosystem services
for the entire world was $33 trillion per year. By now it must be at
least double that.

Wang Li: The good side is that it puts a clear and enormous value on the living world that must be accounted for. The
downside is that it suggests everything is subject to cost-benefit
analysis.

Bob Irving: What's the value you can put on extinction of species
that don't provide any apparent or measurable ecosystem services?

Ruth Johnson: Yes, what? Yes, other than what someone would
pay for it. But that's lunacy.

Wang Li: An ecosystem was defined in the 1992 Convention on
Biological Diversity as: "a dynamic complex of plant, animal, and
micro-organism communities and their non-living environment
interacting as a functional unit."

Bob Irving: I bet they didn't stop there.

Wang Li: No, they didn't. They unleashed the accountants,
economists, and ecologists and disaggregated what the living world
brings to us in an attempt to properly respect and value it.

Bob Irving: I can't wait.

Wang Li: The Millennium Ecosystem Assessment (2003) has
four types of ecosystem services to value: Provisioning Services, the
necessities we consume like food, water, wood, fiber, biochemicals,
genetic resources; Regulating Services that provide us with a habitable environment, regulating climate, disease, water, water purifi-
cation, and pollination; Cultural Ecosystem Services that provide
nonmaterial benefits like religion and spirituality; recreation, eco-
tourism, education, inspiration, sense of place and cultural heritage; Support Services that are needed for the other three like soil
formation, nutrient recycling, and photosynthesis and other forms
of primary production.

Bob Irving: My head is spinning faster on how to put a monetary value on religion and my cultural heritage.

Wang Li: It's priceless. Thought experiment: What price would I be willing to put on my Chinese culture? Obviously, many, many things are priceless.

Ruth Johnson: Yes. My foremother was a Cherokee woman who walked off the Trail of Tears and found refuge in the hills of Tennessee. She lost her heritage as well as her land. It was something my family didn't want to talk about. Don't go there, they said, when I looked at her picture as obviously an Indian woman among the other Anglo members of the Johnson family, all wearing best dresses in a photo of an outdoor family gathering. Cultural destruction was another of the wounds of banishment and ethnic cleansing. The kids on the reservation were often sent to schools that taught only English and did whatever they could to destroy their culture.

Phil Clark: Once upon a time, I was in a small town in Yugoslavia on the Dalmatian coast, when there used to be a Yugoslavia. American television with people watching Peyton Place with Serbo-Croatian subtitles was the collective entertainment in local taverns. Men were also learning to drive and were now able to buy small compact cars and have available running hot water in their houses for showers and dish washing. There did not seem to be much resistance to the short or long-term cultural or ecological consequences. In a world without private cars and good roads and with poor maps, there were often debates over if I could drive to a neighboring town in the mountains or not. Suddenly, I realized that reaching a town ten or fifteen miles away was like traveling to another country across a perilous border. These modern fossil fuel powered transformations were generally enthusiastically welcomed. We were more modern, richer, more comfortable, or so it seemed. Thinking about natural capital, if it was considered at all, seemed to be a distraction and a luxury for the rich.

Bob Irving: "Paved paradise and put up a parking lot…"

Sam Morrison: And the consequences are that now even the rich will become, in various ways, impoverished and limited as a consequence of wealth and pillage.

Wang Li: Of course, the first response of the rich is to say to those late to the party, slow down so that we, the mega-consuming class, preserve our way of life.

Ruth Johnson: A spectacular failure particularly given the globalization of markets and the relentless drive for profits from low-waged production with little regard to ecological and social consequences.

Wang Li: Thus, China becomes a global factory. And, at the same time, global leader in solar and wind. It's only by having clear ecological market rules and price signals that we can begin to make global market systems respond to ecological reality. International ecological discipline can be imposed by ecological tariffs on goods and services noncompliant with ecological market rules.

Bob Irving: Yes. We must value natural capital and ecosystems services in a world run by accountants and corporations. Unless things have explicit value, they are considered valueless, and therefore can be ignored. Positively, it's an attempt to guide and to educate and to account for everything that matters in determining the all-powerful bottom line so beloved by Mr. Market. I'm a contractor. When things have a value, a price tag, they count in the stream of things and purchases, and therefore my bookkeeping and inventory. It's what I book on my balance sheet that literally means what I count. So we must value ecology, sustainability, and restoration of ecosystems, not as consumable stocks like piles of lumber, but as what really counts that ends up on the balance sheet. The real paid in capital must include the ecological value preserved and supported.

Pentti Aalto: Otherwise it's pretending that when you are making money at the same time you are polluting, depleting, and destroying ecosystems, you are increasing entropy, damaging what cannot be easily recovered, and this represents a real loss, not profit. Ecosystem services is a kluge in engineering terms, an awkward attempt to cobble together something that works given existing circumstances. What we need, as you say, is a way to value ecological improvement to be monetized as both paid in capital and as cash.

Ruth Johnson: Yes, it feels sacrilegious to talk about preserving ecological value as being expressed as paid in capital and as cash on balance sheets. Yet, the more I think of this, it's correct as Bob has said, we do not pay too much attention to things without a price tag attached.

5. Monetizing & Restoring Green Capital

Sam Morrison: Yes, we've left the garden. We've lost more than our innocence by eating from the tree of knowledge of good and bad. I think what we lost was not happy innocence, but our instinctive understanding of the harmony of all things. What we gained was the knowledge to act in ways that can be self-serving and self-destructive. The good news is that the Green Republic can in fact offer something quite new under the sun.

Phil Clark: New postal manuals of rules and regs and the bureaucrats to enforce them?

Sam Morrison: Much more than that. A way, a new way, of not only valuing but effectively monetizing ecological value and sustainability. Very real and very practically, we can value sustainability. We can monetize, for example, the ecological value of displacement of one metric ton of carbon dioxide emissions by renewable energy. This is valued at one hundred dollars per metric ton by the US National Academy of Sciences.

Pentti Aalto: This is an attempt to reconcile market forces with preserving and increasing ecological value. It's not a moral exhortation, but it is a serious attempt to radically transform the terms of the debate. It attempts to reconcile and align economic conduct with ecological restoration. No small feat if we can accomplish this. Monetizing—turning ecological improvement into money on balance sheets—is what the financial system of an ecological civilization must accomplish.

Bob Irving: So. Let me understand. One hundred bucks a ton for what?

Phil Clark: Each kilowatt hour of power generated in the US emits on average about one pound of carbon dioxide. Each 2,204-kilowatt hours produce one metric ton of carbon dioxide. Our familiar English ton is two thousand pounds. A metric tonne is one thousand kilograms, or 2,204 pounds.

Pentti Aalto: Each 2,204-kilowatt hours of solar or wind generation is ecologically valued for the ton of carbon dioxide displaced at one hundred dollars by the National Academy of Sciences.

Bob Irving: So what? How do I make that into money and move markets?

Pentti Aalto: It's the creation of a new store of value. The new gold. But creating monetary value from the consequence of actions that protect and restore the living world, so-called natural capital.

Phil Clark: The NAS has taken the first step and put a dollar value on the ecological benefits of displacing a metric ton of carbon dioxide. What his means globally is there's about thirty-five billion tons of carbon dioxide emissions a year. That's $3.5 trillion in ecological value potential ever year from carbon displacement. It's not a one year thing, each year generating renewable energy that displaces or prevents one metric ton of carbon dioxide pollution is valued at one hundred dollars.

Pentti Aalto: And the next step is to create a regulatory asset, a Sustainability Credit or (SC) based on the one-hundred-dollar monetary value of displacing a metric ton of carbon by renewable energy. There are already other regulatory assets, like Solar Renewable Energy Credits (SRECs) that can have an assigned dollar value and are required to be purchased by commercial energy suppliers to be able to meet the required minimum percentage of renewable energy in their portfolios.

Phil Clark: But SRECs are quite different. They are required to be purchased by power suppliers and raise prices like a tax. But SCs are different. They create value, serving as the new gold.

Pentti Aalto: The SCs produced by renewable energy producers ranging from big-time developers to people with a single solar panel as individuals or as organized community associations or coops. It's important that this isn't just for the rich. Solar panels become not just energy generation devices, but means for capital and asset building.

Sam Morrison: SCs are turned to money on the books of a Green Investment Bank or a Bank of the Commons. The bank certifies the renewable energy production, and since it's metered, that's not hard.

Phil Clark: And then here's the magic that's an unanticipated benefit of investment banking. The one hundred dollars for each SC becomes paid in capital on the balance sheet on the right or liability side and as cash on the left or asset side. The right side is capital invested or borrowed. The left side cash assets from SCs is used to make further loans to finance renewable development.

Pentti Aalto: Here's the sweet spot. If a Bank of the Commons has $10 million in SCs on its books, the bank can now loan $90–100 million in new renewable projects.

Bob Irving: Huh?

Pentti Aalto: The magic of banking means a bank needs to keep around 10 percent or less of owned assets to cover their loans. Keep one dollar to secure nine to ten dollars in loans.

Sam Morrison: Let's not get lost in the financial weeds now. But $3.5 trillion yearly global potential in SCs means the potential capacity to create $35 trillion a year to invest in the transformation of our industrial to an ecological civilization through the use of these Sustainability Credits (SCs) based on displacement or sequestering of carbon dioxide. And that's $35 trillion every year for new investment in sustainability. That means, in effect, the major question is how fast can we build the global renewable energy infrastructure with abundant capital for productive ecological investment.

Ruth Johnson: The SCs by their nature are a tool to do both good and well. Usually, those two impulses to increase profits and decrease ecological pillage are in conflict and do not align. Here the profit incentive is through ecological improvement monetized and banked and used for further multiples of ecological investment. And the more we do this, the more these renewables displace carbon, the more money created, the more restoration of habitat.

Bob Irving: Have we squared the circle?

Phil Clark: Maybe. And this means that the $50 trillion that JPMorgan Chase estimated would cost to go to 100 percent renewable globally from 2020 to 2050 could be generated through Sustainability Credits no problem, and much faster than thirty-one years.

Ruth Johnson: That's a real opportunity to save ourselves from global climate disaster through productive ecological investment implemented as fast as we can.

Pentti Aalto: Could this melt the heart of market haters? And make the pursuit of ecological value and improvement the dominant business value proposition.

Sam Morrison: Maybe. And this is productive investment that produces jobs and slashes pollution, depletion, and ecological damage. The paradigmatic example of economic growth leading to ecological improvement. What's crucial to understand is that assigning value on balance sheets to ecology protected and sustained changes the economic calculus. There are enormous amounts of dollar values that can be produced and reinvested in further ecological improvement. Over time, hundreds of trillions of dollars can be produced to finance the ecological transformation. This is real, productive investment in renewables that both produce energy and create ecological value. It's not just running printing presses. It's productive investment building the renewable energy infrastructure hiring workers and generating zero fuel cost renewables. The monetary consequences can be managed by the Federal Reserve or other relevant central banks using familiar means to further expand or contract the money supply as the situation requires.

Bob Irving: So protecting the ecosphere is the Green Republic's path toward ecological economic growth and good jobs at good wages. Real green money. Who would have thought that high finance and financial engineering could be a hallmark of building an ecological civilization and stopping climate change?

Sam Morrison: Yes. Strange but true.

Bob Irving: Sign me up.

Ruth Johnson: So there is something new under the sun that we are considering. Real dollars and sense. To coin a pun.

Sam Morrison: It has been an article of faith and fact since the industrial revolution and its "dark Satanic Mills," as aptly labeled by Blake, to today's Deep Green radicals that industrial civilization and economic growth is inextricably linked with ecological destruction. But we are arguing that within the context of a Green Republic, there are measures that reverse this march to self-destruction and, in fact, can make seeking profit also the practice of ecological restoration if done just so.

Bob Irving: Yes. If there are real dollars and cents on the table, then Section Two of Article One is important because it's affirmatively result oriented. "Economic activity in this Republic shall be guided by principles under law that lead to the improvement and regeneration of natural capital and the advancement of social and ecological justice." It says that my work will be judged by consequences.

Pentti Aalto: Section Three is good in that it clearly is meant not to let the bean counters off the hook. There's no escape hatch that's says we are all in support of ecological conduct, but now down to business and our responsibilities to make bucks above all else.

Wang Li: Regulation is aspiration unless enforced.

Phil Clark: Agreed. This is just the framework. And what exactly, pray tell, do we really mean by "the advancement of social and ecological justice?"

6. Justice Always Justice

Sam Morrison: I believe our current common sense of justice is "justice as fairness." This is most clearly identified today by the philosopher John Rawls.

Ruth Johnson: There's also the deep spiritual sense, from Amos: "But let justice roll down like waters. And righteousness like an ever-flowing stream."

Sam Morrison: Justice is social. It's more than the Golden Rule, do unto others as you would have them do unto you. Or as Hillel offered as his capsule summary of the Torah, "What is hateful to you, do not do unto others."

Phil Clark: Hillel's interpretation is closer to Kant's sense of a categorical imperative to be practiced by all since Hillel is focusing on others, not just on personal consequences.

Sam Morrison: And to put this in ecological terms we might say, "Do unto the earth as the earth will do unto us."

Pentti Aalto: This is a reasonably clear sense for social and ecological justice.

Ruth Johnson: Justice is fairness and rooted in consequences both personal and ecological. It encompasses and transcends the personal and is understood socially and ecologically.

Phil Clark: Justice as fairness has the advantage of being able to pass the test advanced by John Rawls of personal ignorance of your starting position in order to evaluate the justice or the fairness of actions. If we do not know if we have skin in the game or not, we can more objectively judge the justice of action.

Sam Morrison: It's a departure from Plato who found justice as properly serving your predetermined role in the grand hierarchy ruled by the guardian philosopher kings. While "do your job" applies to football today, it's no longer understood as the basis and touchstone for justice.

Phil Clark: I think you're riding too quickly over virtue, education, and the hard dynamics of power and choice. I think Plato's *Republic* wrestled hard with the question of how those with the role and weight of leadership struggled to get things right, and for whom the question of justice, not greed or glory, was central. These matters were addressed to thinking wise men, and women—yes women too, not just to Spartan men. Justice was on the table.

Sam Morrison: Yes. I bow my head before the great philosopher, as well as the importance for the Green Republic to embrace the issues of justice in social and ecological terms. Awareness of social and ecological justice and education about its central importance is crucial to the purpose of the Green Republic. And thus, we follow the master Plato's path up the winding rocky hill clinging to the saddle pommel, almost falling, rocking back and forth, losing sight of the trail for moments, but moving on.

Phil Clark: Humility enters, along with Plato.

Sam Morrison: Yes, it does. At least sticks its nose in the tent.

Phil Clark: It's importance to also consider that justice for Rawls was a focus for rational individual decisions—it was scarcely viewed in practice as an expression of community. "Community" is not even in the index of *A Theory of Justice*. This is liberalism as philosophy applied to justice.

Wang Li: And liberalism is knotted up with markets and class, the tiny, rich owners/rulers and the growing poor and impoverished, within the context of wealth accumulated typically through ecological pillage, or at least indifference.

Sam Morrison: It's not that Rawls thought community unimportant, but that his sense of justice was much more rooted in personal choices within the context of an imagined liberal social contract, and the reasoned decisions by individuals rather than a product of the ongoing push and pull of freedom and community to find a sustainable balance. That's what a Green Republic is about.

Phil Clark: That standpoint of the gentleman ...

Wang Li: Or gentlewoman ...

Phil Clark: Or gentlewoman in her drawing room, or the Harvard Club cogitating and deciding upon the proper decision is quite different than the interpenetration, the swirl of freedom and community, of the one and the many that is characterized by ecosystems in motion and social life. We are subject to all kinds of influences—from the past that shapes our reality, and in the present—that push and pull, that influence our lives and choices.

Sam Morrison: We are closer to the flock in the air turning almost simultaneously on the basis of well-developed mirror neurons that pick up and respond quickly to subtle changes, evolutionarily selected for their survival value. And language and writing provide an enormously strong form of social mirroring, response, and choice by humans. This is not just a matter of individual choice, but a social phenomenon.

Pentti Aalto: Language, of course, is meaningless without the social. What
characterizes the most telling fact of our species is also the most resolutely social phenomena—language—and the most useful to inspire sudden and dramatic action by others shared and communicated by an idea. That's a rather awe-inspiring concept. The animal that acts and communicates at a great distance and at great intervals of time on the basis of an idea.

Ruth Johnson: It's worth being aware of the distinction that justice in the Green Republic is rooted in rights and responsibilities for fair and sustainable conduct, and not just for satisfying the needs of the dominant hierarchy and feeding the megamachine. Justice is conditioned and shaped by explicit ecological ends. Justice is not an isolated and abstract concept. For a Green Republic, justice is explicitly social and ecological. This recognizes that the social and the ecological, like freedom and community, are interdependent, and the one cannot thrive without the other. Without ecological justice, social justice is undermined and will ultimately collapse. Without social justice, the ability to pursue ecological justice in the long term is thoroughly undermined.

Pentti Aalto: And it's also worth remembering that the issues of getting things right, the successful pursuit of sustainability for us is the triumph of justice which has a particular manifestation for our times.

Wang Li: And the challenge of implementation and renewing balance of a sustainable ecological order is more than the adoption of a program we are presenting. It's more than technique. It's the social manifestation of justice in our time, and that is dependent upon the virtue of the citizens and their education and the great social conversation and the development and application of an ecological common sense.

Phil Clark: That's a kind of world spirit for the time. A belief in what we learn and, over time, intuitively and collectively know what it means to be just and fair.

Bob Irving: Like one person, one vote. Not one dollar, one vote.

Phil Clark: Like social and ecological justice manifest through the pursuit of sustainability.

Wang Li: Where does this leave us?

Phil Clark: With a greater suspicion—no, a real understanding—that method alone, that prescriptive changes alone, will not save us.

Pentti Aalto: Like Eugene Debs, the old socialist who said, if I could lead you to the promised land, I wouldn't, because if I could lead you in, someone else could lead you out.

Phil Clark: Hence a grand social movement of an ecological turn that engages all aspects of our lives and civilization where we have to build the road as we travel.

Bob Irving: And we have to keep building quickly.

Wang Li: The ice is melting.

Bob Irving: Now's the time.

Phil Clark: The prospects of a coming execution concentrates the mind.

Pentti Aalto: I certainly hope so.

Ruth Johnson: Where does this leave us.

Phil Clark: Back to the question at hand.

Sam Morrison: It's important to understand in this broad context that Article One: Ecological Conduct is by itself is necessary, but not sufficient for the effective pursuit of sustainability. Both in terms of philosophic scope and practical effect.

Phil Clark: Yes. On the practical application side, only Article One, Section 3 on defining fiduciary responsibility for decision makers sends clear signals in advance to markets and beyond.

Ruth Johnson: This has broader resonance, as well, in terms of scope. The imperatives for ecological conduct, for the pursuit of social and ecological justice, must be explicit and function to send clear signals throughout the economy and society for decisions on production, consumption, and investments by government, by business, by institutions, and individuals.

Wang Li: Obviously the complexity of decisions in a market economy with myriad decisions to invest, to produce, to purchase is driven by the price system. Getting the price system to send clear signals for sustainability is key.

Pentti Aalto: Technique and method here rubs against some broader themes as well.

Phil Clark: Technique is always changing. So if we have a list of twenty things, soon there can be twenty-five different things to replace the first twenty. We need to be aware that principles can be manifest through different techniques.

Ruth Johnson: We're not saying that technology, or market rules, don't matter, but that any particular method is just one variation upon a principle that can be manifest in many ways.

7. Globalization of Sustainability

Sam Morrison: We now have a pile of numbers describing a mountain of new machines.

Phil Clark: Hello Meagan. Good to see you. Woman of the orchid bees, how are the hives?

Meagan Simons: All is buzzing. Like we are now.

Bob Irving: Yes. Out with the old. In with the new. Industrialization transformed by producing new benign machines. Is that what's the Green Republic has come down to?

Meagan Simons: A Green Republic is a social, political, economic, and philosophical innovation. It's not just a new pile of machines. It's all about a new way of living.

Pentti Aalto: Yes, it embraces new technological manifestations to produce, for instance, many trillions of kilowatt hours of efficient renewable electricity a year.

Phil Clark: That's not a trivial undertaking.

Ruth Johnson: No. It is not. It makes me think sometimes about unwinding this. A civilization built upon artful survival and low impact and not this throbbing global high technology hive. How do we make the choices to live artfully, sustainably, not driven by consumption fevers of the already rich?

Phil Clark: I think we're in too deep to pretend we can simply return to the preindustrialized age and this time start from zero and get it right. But in another sense, that's what an ecological civilization and the pursuit of sustainability is all about, getting it right this time. To live is a world that's both ecological and high techno-logical is a new challenge.

Ruth Johnson: The truth of the matter are social decisions in the context of social and ecological justice. This means, over time, a global convergence on sustainable norms manifest in things like a guaranteed annual income for all, a sustainable three tons of carbon dioxide emissions per person per year, a fair share of the social product, reduction in necessary work hours and increase in social energy, of love and pleasure. In a society where we all have access to good food, clean air and water, education, health care, housing, leisure, retirement, safe productive work, and participation in the ownership and governance of all the institutions from work to school to hospital guided by the ecological and social justice imperative, we can start to make real decisions.

Wang Li: It means that we must consciously engage with and accept the responsibilities that accompany our freedom to develop such technological power and complexity.

Pentti Aalto: The world used 157,000 terawatts of primary energy in 2018. About a third of that is wasted and final useful energy out is around 104,000 terawatt hours. There's a billion kilowatt hours in a terawatt. So the challenge is what we use and how we produce it. Around 85 percent of that currently comes from fossil fuels, and much of that is wasted. The second law of efficiency is spectacularly poor.

Phil Clark: Fossil fueled industrial civilization was built on prodigal fossil fuel energy use in a low efficiency, high pollution economy. The challenge we face is to come to terms with, as a rapidly as we can, a transformation from a high waste, high pollution fossil fuel economy to a low waste, low pollution, high efficiency renewable economy. The fossil fuel world is based on huge amounts of waste in every stage. An efficient renewable world, by contrast, takes advantage of second law efficiencies whenever possible, getting the most nonpolluting work or energy out for the minimal amount of energy in.

Bob Irving: Wait a minute. I know a little about the second law. But for most people I deal with, as far as they know, the first law is don't pick up the heavy end, and the second law is don't park on the railroad tracks.

Phil Clark: In plain non-physicist English, you can't easily put toothpaste back into the tube once it's squirted out. For example, most of the energy from gasoline in an internal combustion engine ends up as heat from hot exhaust gases, or heat from friction to turn the driveshaft, the gears and the wheels, energy to run fuel pumps and other hardware. Only about 17–21 percent of the available energy in gasoline is kinetic energy actually used to move the mass of the car. An electric car is the opposite, 77 percent efficient with regenerative braking. No hot gases, fewer moving parts. The second law efficiency, useful energy out compared to energy in, is more than three-and-a-half times better for electric vehicles.

Bob Irving: What that means is cost for running electrics is about one dollar per gallon equivalent. That gets my attention.

Pentti Aalto: The classic efficiency story beyond cars is substitution of heat pumps that take heat out of the air to replace fossil fuel boilers. Right now, you can get three to four units of useful heat energy out on a seasonal basis of each unit of renewable electricity in. Solar energy heats the air and the ground. You take that free heat and through a compressor, take advantage of the Carnot cycle and get three kilowatt hours of useful energy out compared to the one kilowatt of energy you used to run the compressor. And the theoretical maximum efficiency of such a system is over twenty to one.

Phil Clark: Material sciences and nanotech are moving us in the direction of vastly more efficient machines. And if energy and the consequences of its use included the real costs of pollution, depletion, and ecological damage, we would be pursuing the low waste solution.

Pentti Aalto: Right now, we can reasonably aspire to increase overall efficiency by a factor of tree. The world uses 157,000 terawatt hours of primary Energy becomes 52,333 terawatt hours, and in the not-too-distant twenty-second century future, improve efficiency by a factor of ten and use 15,700 terawatt hours of smart and efficient renewable energy. That would include green hydrogen produced by solar power electrolyzers.

Ruth Johnson: The Green Republic is all about wrestling with these questions and their implications. The first thing is to engage the shape of the problem. The fossil fuel age must end as quickly as possible, before it takes us with it in its death throes.

Bob Irving: It sounds like we have to lean a great deal on the scientists and engineers to get this done.

Sam Morrison: The fundamental question is not technical. There are technical questions for sure. But the fundamental issue is to what ends and for what purpose are we building and employing these technologies.

Ruth Johnson: Are we following the mandates of Article One: The Ecological Imperative, or are we mortgaging and destroying our future for some quick and dirty profits until the music stops playing?

Wang Li: The continuation of business and pollution as usual will mean we will find ourselves at the mercy of the situation we have created.

Meagan Simons: Our task is starting from where we are and rebuilding the shape of our civilization, not just with new machines, but with a deliberate and conscious pursuit of social and ecological justice, new life-ways to accomplish this, and the regeneration of natural capital.

Sam Morrison: This is the life shape of the Green Republic. It about building a new way we can live. It's predicated on not just a single Green Republic as a sustainable island in a polluted sea.

Phil Clark: So the Green Republic is a model for a sustainable globalization.

Sam Morrison: Yes, that in a broad sense is correct. It's not to be a duplicate cookie-cutter, but it's the manifestation of a powerful social innovation, a meme that can spread, be adapted, and evolve, and changed to fit varied circumstances.

Phil Clark: I've hated that word meme as a social substitute for gene. Meaning it carries the essence of an idea. And worse is to use it like Dawkins's notion of the selfish gene whose function or behavior is to reproduce itself.

Wang Li: Agreed. We don't need to go down that road. There's meme as expression of the healing social response to excess, not a meme as a social gene.

Sam Morrison: Meme as social innovation and purpose that can be a basis for the global spread of sustainability and the social construction of an ecological civilization.

Meagan Simons: In his book *Sapiens: A Brief History of Humankind*, Yuval Harari wrote, "We control the word basically because we are the only animals that can cooperate flexibly in very large numbers. And...you will always find that it is based on some fiction like the nation, like money, like human rights. These are all things that do not exist objectively, but they exist only in the stories that we tell and spread around. This is something very unique to us, perhaps the most unique feature of our species."

Wang Li: The Green Republic is about planting and nurturing the seeds for a global social revolution, to build a sustainable ecological civilization from the current industrial reality. Its focus is local, but the consequences are global.

Sam Morrison: Yes. We are talking about a healing globalization with sustainability as an animating and motivating concept for a conscious human response to ecological pillage and crisis. A Green Republic employs a new generation of technological tools. But the purpose is to use these tools in the pursuit of sustainability, of social and ecological justice, and the regeneration and health of the ecosphere and all its inhabitants.

8. Three Tons of Carbon Dioxide Per Person Per Year

Phil Clark: As a physicist, there's something we need to be clear about from the start. There are some physical and clearly measurable and quantifiable manifestations of what a Green Republic, or any competing alternative, must accomplish. And it's not even rocket science.

Bob Irving: The acid test, so to speak.

Phil Clark: Simply, the average amount of carbon dioxide released per person per year on the planet of seven billion of us must be no more than three tons per person per year. For seven billion people, that's twenty-one gigatons of carbon. That's three tons per person maximum after carbon dioxide levels are stabilized at levels substantially below four hundred parts per million. Carbon dioxide has now increased to over four hundred parts per million and rising from the preindustrial 280 parts per million levels of carbon dioxide.

Pentti Aalto: This means in practical terms we need to replace the fossil fuel infrastructure almost entirely, reduce emissions to the lowest possible level, and then reduce existing carbon dioxide through soil building, sustainable agricultural practices, and reforestation.

Bob Irving: And if the population is eight or nine billion, then three tons per person doesn't cut it. If we have nine billion people, the average individual carbon entitlement drops to 2.3 tons per person per year unless we pull carbon from atmosphere and ocean and sequester in biomass and soil.

Phil Clark: Twenty-one gigatons of anthropogenic emissions is the limit more or less to maintain the existing global carbon balance. Of course, as we acidify the oceans, which dissolves atmospheric carbon dioxide into carbonic acid, there are unpleasant consequences like dissolving the skeletons of plankton that turns carbon dioxide into oxygen that could affect processes of global carbon balance.

Bob Irving: That does not sound good.

Phil Clark: You bet. Reducing the global circular flow of carbon dioxide used by marine organisms to replenish atmospheric oxygen at some point will unleash major and disruptive ecological changes in oceans and on land globally. That's more in Sam's and Meagan's area of expertise. What I can say is that a population of nine billion would either cut the individual allowance for carbon dioxide 2.3 tons or increase the amount of carbon dioxide sequestered in soil and biomass on land and on sea to keep the three tons per person per year standard.

Sam Morrison: To be clear. Stop building all new fossil fuel plants and shut down the old ones as soon as we can.

Bob Irving: And what's significant about twenty-one gigatons of carbon dioxide compared to, say, twenty-five or fifteen?

Phil Clark: Twenty-one gigatons of carbon dioxide a year is equal to the annual natural sinks for carbon in the oceans, soil, plant matter, and photosynthesis that keeps atmospheric carbon concentrations level. This is a central challenge for a Green Republic and all of humanity globally in the twenty-first century and beyond. We must first stabilize the percentage of carbon dioxide in the atmosphere, now over four hundred parts per million and increasing, and, second, reverse this toward the preindustrial levels of around 280 parts per million.

Pentti Aalto: Even if we reduced emissions to twenty-one gigatons of carbon, the three tons per person per year, we'd still be at dangerous levels in the 450 to 500 ppm range. We'd need to pursue agricultural and forestry practices that remove carbon dioxide from the atmosphere and slash methane emissions. This is called a global cooling agenda by Hans Joseph Fell. Carbon dioxide from the atmosphere to the soil and woody biomass. Methane not leaking from natural gas wells and not produced by industrialized meat production, and not generated by rotting organic waste streams without enough oxygen—anaerobic digestion. Instead, aerobic composting, with enough oxygen, produces good soil, not CH_4—that's methane. It means aerating by turning the compost pile or other methods of getting oxygen in from active or passive by design.

Bob Irving: You mean air holes or air tube in the composter. Or take my manure fork and turn the pile every few days when I check out the garden.

Pentti Aalto: Yes, like that.

Sam Morrison: The trajectory and intent is the path toward zero emissions, to replace entirely the fossil fuel energy structure with renewables, and to adopt sustainable norms and practices for agriculture and forestry, not to walk the line between sustainability and ecological catastrophe. But twenty-one gigatons is the absolute red light. If a very small and consistent annual increase in atmospheric carbon dioxide will mean the penalty will over time be catastrophic.

Bob Irving: The alternative to the sustainable is the catastrophic. We don't get to reliably choose the not-so-bad, or accurately forecast how quickly the catastrophe will happen. If I build a house and don't design the roof, porch, and the soffit vent system properly, if the weather's just right—or wrong—you'll get ice dams. In a winter with alternating snowing, melting, and freezing, the ice dams will keep growing, and at some point, leaks will start, and at some point after x tons if ice accumulate, the roof will give way.

Phil Clark: Like the winter collapse at the Hartford Coliseum.

Bob Irving: Exactly.

Wang Li: What happens in far from equilibrium condition is subject to chaotic dynamics subject to the influence of strange attractors that are anything but linear.

Phil Clark: The rather astounding thing is that twenty-one giga-tons of carbon dioxide a year and three tons per person per year means nothing to almost everyone in practice. If we were taking climate change and sustainability seriously, the three tons would be almost as familiar to every citizen as fifty states in the union, 714 home runs by Babe Ruth, and April 15 is Tax Day.

Bob Irving: Keeping it simple, to one measure, the percentage of atmospheric carbon dioxide is the canary in the coal mine for irreversible global ecological crisis. Not the only one that matters, for sure. But a crucial measure. And if we don't succeed?

Phil Clark: If we don't stop the increase of carbon dioxide at some point, and we're not sure exactly where this point is—at 450 or 500 or 550 or 600 or 650 or 700 parts per million—geophysical forces make climate change irreversible from melting ice decreasing the earth's albedo.

Bob Irving: What's that?

Phil Clark: Sorry. That's the amount of sunlight reflected back into space by snow and ice instead of heating the ground and the oceans. So if the ice vanishes from the Arctic ocean in the summer, enormous amounts of heat pour into the oceans. And for the already warming oceans, this will accelerate the release of methane into the atmosphere, from melting methane hydrates from perma-frost and warming sea bottoms, gigatons of a greenhouse gas that's at least twenty-three times more potent than carbon dioxide ... And there's more, but you get the idea that we risk falling into the grasp of geophysical forces that could mean roughly recapitulating the Eocene Thermal Maximum lasting hundreds of thousands of years. Trust me, we don't want to go there.

Ruth Johnson: In mythic terms, it's like the biblical tale of the flood. Only worse.

Phil Clark: Only much worse. And not to depress you, but carbon dioxide isn't our only concern. Natural gas. That's methane—chemically, CH_4—that's promoted as a bridge to a sustainable world may, in fact, make matters worse or no better.

Bob Irving: We might as well face the music.

9. Natural Gas: Part of the Problem, Not the Solution

Phil Clark: Natural gas may produce less carbon per megawatt of capacity than coal *if* you can prevent almost all fugitive methane from leaking into the atmosphere. Methane is at least twenty-three times more potent of a greenhouse gas than carbon dioxide. It's the small sloppy methane leaks, not just the catastrophic well blowouts. The further bad news about methane is that in the short run, over ten years, it's much worse than carbon.

Bob Irving: Worse than carbon?

Phil Clark: Yes, in the short run it has much more global warming potential.

A carbon molecule hangs out for up to several hundred thousand years in the atmosphere. Sixty-five to 80 percent dissolves in the ocean over twenty to two hundred years. The rest then is removed very slowly by chemical weathering and rock formation. Methane is much more chemically reactive and is mostly gone in twelve years.

Pentti Aalto: So the significance of methane release, like the California Aliso Canyon explosion, is important. Over 112 days, one hundred thousand tons of methane poured into the atmosphere. That released the equivalent of the greenhouse gases from half a million cars. It was the second-largest point source of greenhouse gases in the US, after an Alabama coal mine. Plus, lots of carcinogens like toluene.

Phil Clark: Remember, 74 percent of total greenhouse gases are carbon dioxide. But the warming potential of methane in the short run is enormous. Carbon molecules outnumber methane molecules five to one in the atmosphere. But over a ten-year period, methane traps over fifty times more heat than carbon dioxide. According to NASA's Goddard Institute for Space Studies, a methane molecule released today is one hundred times more heat-trapping than a molecule of carbon dioxide.

Bob Irving: As a countryman, I know that much of human related methane comes, by the way, from cow burps in agricultural feed lots.

Phil Clark: The good news, by the way, was that for the US at least, methane releases had been decreasing. The bad news is that the turn to natural gas means that methane releases are expected to increase markedly from the oil and natural gas sector.

Wang Li: The well cap is plugged in California, but the Alabama coal plants legally chug on.

Ruth Johnson: And will before we stop it.

Phil Clark: The basic points here are first, natural gas is not an effective global warming substitute for coal. If methane is included, it may even be worse than coal. And, in any case, a new gas plant is just pouring more carbon into the atmosphere, albeit at a slowed rate per megawatt. Second, if we are concerned with climate change, stop building any more fossil fuel plants and shut down the existing ones, ASAP. Third, methane is a menace whose human linked production is primarily from cows raised for meat, from landfills, and from natural gas drilling.

Bob Irving: The true price of steak and landfills and natural gas is unaffordable.

Phil Clark: Aerobic composting of food waste, manure, and wastewater needs to be systematically applied. Existing landfills should capture and burn methane for energy. This is the only sensible large-scale use of natural gas to replace coal. We need, as well, to wean ourselves from industrialized meat and dairy production.

Bob Irving: Yes, Beyond Meat veggie burgers. Not bad. Food science that can make veggie inputs taste bloody like real meat.

Phil Clark: And fourth, the climate and ecological effects of agriculture and forestry are enormous and must be a part of that ecological transformation that must affect all aspects of our lives.

Sam Morrison: And we should turn to green hydrogen from solar powered electrolyzers to turn water into hydrogen and oxygen to either power combustion turbines to produce lots of power quickly to balance a renewable energy grid, or feed the hydrogen into existing natural gas pipelines.

Wang Li: I read this year at Fukushima they just opened the world's largest solar powered electrolyzer powered by a ten-megawatt solar farm supplying green hydrogen to a combustion turbine on site that feeds power into the Japanese power grid taking advantage of the power lines built once upon a time for the Fukushima nuclear complex.

Bob Irving: It's like being a volunteer firefighter in my town. First, there's chaos and emergency when you show up at a site. Are there any people to be saved? Any animals? Anything like propane tanks or a meth lab that may explode? Second, there's a process—reduce the heat, knock down the temperature, cut off the oxygen and the fuel. We have our Fire Service Procedures. So we'll have our procedures for climate change and an ecological future. The farmers, the foresters, the waste people, the power guys will all have their proper procedures, and we'll all learn what's good practice and what's not. And this will change and evolve all the time as we get better and tackle more and more aspects of the problem. For natural gas, knock down the meat and dairy production.

Pentti Aalto: The climate and ecological effects of agriculture and forestry are enormous and must be a part of that ecological transformation that must affect all aspects of our lives.

Ruth Johnson: It feels like we've opened my aunt's closet and all kinds of things just came spilling out and I don't know what to pick up first.

Pentti Aalto: And to my market mind, that speaks of much opportunity and productive investment that makes economic growth lead to ecological improvement.

Ruth Johnson: We hope.

Phil Clark: Yes, we do.

10. THREE TONS PER PERSON IN NATIONAL AND GLOBAL PERSPECTIVE

Wang Li: A Green Republic is about addressing what three tons per person per year of carbon means combined with global cooling activities from soil building and forestry by both rich and poor nations. Global per capita total energy use was in 2012 was 4.5 tons of carbon per person per year, a 22,127 kWh equivalent. That doesn't seem like such a big deal. Reduce from 4.5 to 3.0 and then plant more trees and cultivate and enrich the soil differently.

Pentti Aalto: But that's not the whole story.

Wang Li: No, it isn't. US per capita carbon dioxide release in 2017 was equal to 16.2 tons of carbon dioxide, or a 79,315 kWh equivalent, down from 17.6 tons of carbon per person per year, or a 86,203 kWh equivalent. China per capita total energy use in 2017 was 6.9 of tons carbon per person, or a 33,782 kWh equivalent, up from 2012 with 6.2 tons carbon and increasing. On the other hand, the poorest nations already have carbon levels well below three tons per person per year. Cambodia .61 tons person. Cameroon, .3 tons per person, Columbia, 1.9 tons, Ecuador, 2.4 tons, Indonesia, 2.2 tons, India, 1.8 tons.

Phil Clark: Clearly, if all the world's people lived like we do in the US, we would be doomed. China, with four times as many people, is already catching up with the US in total emissions. India's average carbon was 1.5 tons per person in 2011, but increased to 1.8

tons in 2017. India is not far behind China in industrial aspiration that includes using coal as well as photovoltaics.

Ruth Johnson: Let's make it clear, both from the standpoint of justice and from the realm of political possibility, that the solution is not for the already rich, who have created and profited by the problem to continue to pollute as usual, while the aspiring poor do not.

Wang Li: I should also say that China now is a global leader in photovoltaics and wind, and India has also gone all-in on huge solar gigawatt-capacity factories. The challenge is a global convergence on sustainable conduct and prosperity for all. That's the challenge for the Green Republic. We are here to understand the architecture for a Green Republic, and for an accompanying successful global pursuit of sustainability.

Phil Clark: We need to vault over the fossil fuel age into the renewably powered information age. It's interesting to note that 5.1 billion people have cell phones, while 3.8 billion have running water. The point here is we don't need to recapitulate the fossil fuel power grid any more than we need to string telephone wires. The solution is a global ecological turn for renewable power that can help lift the poor and provide all of us with running water and sustainable, low-carbon lives.

Ruth Johnson: And to do so within the context of social and ecological justice.

Phil Clark: What's startling is that we are essentially unaware of the fundamental dynamic of sustainable and unsustainable emissions of carbon dioxide. We have little concept of what it means to reduce emissions to three tons per person per year and change our agricultural and forestry practices to wring excess carbon dioxide from the air. This should be job one for all of us, for everyone in the whole human family. Every one of us. That's social and ecological justice.

Bob Irving: We need to place ourselves on a war footing. Except this time, we are fighting for the long-term survival and prosperity of the human race. For all of us. For all living things. That's our freedom and our responsibility. We spent around 1.91 trillion dollars a year globally on the military in 2019. With the US alone spending about one-third of this. And a lot of that war money, I should add, is spent for wars over the control of oil and natural gas. We also blew 16.8 trillion on the financial bailout in 2007–8 to save the bankers and speculators.

Ruth Johnson: Like many great crimes, we don't know because we really don't want to know and face inconvenient truths. We don't act because it's too threatening to the continuation of business and pollution as usual. Yeah. I think we've answered the start of the why and what questions.

Phil Clark: Indeed. The skeptic in me, that sits alongside the physicist, asks, "How?"

Sam Morrison: That's what our discussions are all about.

Phil Clark: I think you covered in a capsule, the why and the what. Now, we have to address the how.

11. Building an Ecological Future

Ruth Johnson: This is a problem that's a consequence of our global industrialization built upon fossil fuels in a high pollution, high waste global industrial system where energy use and carbon output and economic grew, until recently marched forward in lock step.

Pentti Aalto: Until recently is a sign of hope, and of things to come.

Sam Morrison: Yes, it is. That's what a Green Republic must build upon. Emerging facts and reality. Not just a wish

Ruth Johnson: The problem is the result of the civilization we have built and the written and unwritten rules we have followed. The challenge for the Green Republic is to face this challenge squarely and offer solutions that are fair, just, and democratic and applicable for all.

Phil Clark: The problems of industrial civilization are not reducible to the law-breaking polluters and midnight dumpers. It's the normal, allowable pollution, depletion, and ecological damage.

Sam Morrison: That's the challenge. To look at reality and choose a different path toward sustainability and survival, and, may I add, toward prosperity and peace. It's not a task only for scientists. It's a political, social, economic, and philosophical challenge for us all. Testing whether, as Lincoln asked at Gettysburg, any nation so conceived in liberty can long endure.

Pentti Aalto: There may well be many ways toward sustainability. Since it's technologically feasible, the question is what social pathways lead toward those ends. And all depend on existing conditions. Where we came from. Where we started from. There are all kinds of ideas and thought experiments that have been proposed.

Bob Irving: All over the map that makes my carpenter's head spin. Markets or non-markets, democracy or hierarchy?

Phil Clark: Yes. Speaking of more than three standard deviations from the norm, I've read about things like the Venus project that claims we can solve our problems through an all-encompassing technocracy. Cities designed, built, and managed by engineers for sustainable agriculture and production. City-states without markets and without money. City-states ruled by a benign order of technocrats. Sort of Marx and Engels saying that successful communism would focus on managing things objectively, not people. I don't have faith in markets. And I don't have faith in bureaucrats, technocrats, or politicians either. I'm a college professor. I've experienced the worst of all worlds.

Wang Li: Where's that leave us? Between a rock and a hard place?

Pentti Aalto: Stepping back, as a market man, I got to admit that neither markets nor nonmarkets are by themselves recipes for success. Mr. Market is certainly not the cure for all ills. And we've all heard about market failure, about global market collapses, recessions, and depressions, and about making big profits through ecological pillage.

Phil Clark: There are certainly many species of utopia and dystopia driven by imperatives of necessity to manage and simplify the problem of social life and achieve sustainable conduct. This is true for both so-called free market and for nonmarkets. Like many claims that markets are perfect, except for the small problem of externalities.

Wang Li: Like pollution, depletion, ecological damage, extinction.

Pentti Aalto: Yes. The poisoned fruit of the poisoned tree. In markets and nonmarkets. What's certainly characteristic of many of these thought experiments or historical experiences like Soviet Communism, is that necessity and idealism, untempered by democratic means, tends toward the prospect of dictatorship by one strong man or woman. This gives us a police state, the abuse of power and corruption exercised by an Orwellian inner party. Alternatively, there can be prospects for periods of benign despotism.

Wang Li: And it's also true that unstrained market forces give us global speculative collapse, markets in slaves, markets in extinction for ivory and whales, markets in oil, coal, natural gas, and ecological destruction. Markets without a proper limiting framework are a crippled and blind master.

Bob Irving: I admit that neither markets nor political ideology and politicians are worthy of blind adherence. We are, at best, working at optimizing imperfection. That means hard work. Getting up in the morning and doing what needs to be done, That day and the next. Not saying we have built it and it's good forever.

Ruth Johnson: I think it's safe to say that any system will tend to follow an iron law of oligarchy, that leadership groups will emerge inevitably, and that in systems that are designed as unitary hierarchies, these oligarchies will be deeply, deeply entrenched and tend toward corruption and abuse without the opportunity for countervailing and healing response to excess.

Wang Li: The only healing in entrenched oligarchy comes from internal reform, or revolution. Internal reform, of course, has its risks. The rise of a new leadership group, a Mikhail Gorbachev, for example, whose attempt to reform the unreformable led swiftly toward dissolution of the Soviet system.

Ruth Johnson: This is why President Xi and the Chinese Communist Party do not want to repeat that experience and want to achieve sustainable growth, an end to both ecological degradation and political corruption, the exercise of a rule of law, and the use limited electoral mechanisms all conditioned by the Party and its continuing preeminence.

Pentti Aalto: You could argue that over time the pursuit of such goals would inevitably converge on at least quasi-democratic forms. If exercised fully, there will be the gradual emergence of parties within the party. Instead of factions competing for power organized around powerful leaders.

Phil Clark: It's enormously presumptive to say that the ecologically self-destructive practices of global industrial capitalism and its parliamentary democracies can only be cured by the ministrations of parliamentary democracies. It seems to me like the offering of a renewed license to kill. The rich democracies of the West and the OECD have been the champion polluters, and have historically been responsible for the overwhelming majority of pollution.

12. Global Perspectives and Ecological Glimmerings

Wang Li: According to Greenpeace, from 1960–2005, the US emitted 213.608 gigatons CO_2, 26 percent of total global emissions. The next biggest polluter, China, emitted 88.643 gigatons of CO_2, 10.7 percent of the global total. Per capita, the US emitted 720 tons of CO_2 per person per year from 1960–2005, or sixteen tons per person per year. This is more than ten times China's per capita emissions of sixty-eight tons of CO_2, or 1.5 tons per person per year during the same period, and ninety times the per capita emissions of Kenya of 7.7 tons of CO_2, or .17 tons per person per year. Individually, the fifty US states are among the largest of carbon dioxide emitters. Yes, China has pulled into the lead as the largest emitter at present but has agreed to cap and reduce carbon. It's essential that it does.

Pentti Aalto: Here's some good news before we get too depressed.

Bob Irving: Thanks, I needed that.

Pentti Aalto: In 2020, in the midst of the pandemic, the International Energy Agency (IEA) estimates that primary energy demand in 2020 could decline for oil (–9 percent), coal (–8 percent), natural gas (–5 percent), and nuclear (–2 percent), while renewables would grow by 1 percent. Spending on oil plunged by $1 trillion. Green energy has been resilient but has not reflected the necessary investment growth in the midst of the pandemic.

Sam Morrison: That's the promise of Sustainability Credits (SCs) to align the creation of renewable energy investments with a sustainable ecological recovery from COVID-19 days. SCs means making markets the driver of necessary enormous expansion in renewables and accelerating the renewable transition.

Pentti Aalto: That's a good thing about markets. If you establish a clear and effective value proposition, the markets will aggressively follow that path.

Ruth Johnson: So, Sustainability Credits are just the thing to help save capitalism and the living world from itself and its depredations.

Wang Li: China's carbon emissions are likely to peak by 2022, at least eight years before the 2030 date established for this goal, and this will be followed by progressive reductions, according to Jiang Kejun of the Energy Research Institute division of the National Development and Reform Commission (NDRC). This is very good news. It's crucial to prevent our planet from exceeding a global two-degree-centigrade temperature increase as a result of climate change.

Phil Clark: That's good.

Pentti Aalto: And there's more. Solar systems are already at cost parity with fossil fuels in much of the global market, and the future costs of solar are continuing to drop rapidly. Fossil fuel and nuclear energy will simply not be able to compete with zero fuel cost solar with continuing drops in capital costs per watt and with continuing improvements in output per watt.

Sam Morrison: The bottom line is that to stop exceeding the two-degree-centigrade warming target, if we are fortunate, we need to basically replace much of the existing fossil fuel infrastructure— all the coal plants, for sure—with renewables or non-emitters costing several trillion in productive and profitable capital investment over the next twenty to thirty years and reach our global three tons of carbon per person per year and then start to reduce that.

Wang Li: An ecological turn is in process. It's affordable. It certainly profitable, making economic growth mean ecological improvement. Yes, we are not just looking at energy and carbon. Sustainable practices in agriculture, forestry, aquaculture and fisheries, and industrial ecology, and the health of ecosystems in a zero-pollution, zero-waste production system are all part of what the successful pursuit of sustainability and an ecological civilization must address. Energy and carbon demands our immediate, but certainly not sole, attention.

Phil Clark: But the fossil fuel industry and their purchased politicians shall not go gently into that good night.

Bob Irving: No, they certainly will not. They will lie, bribe, dissemble, sue, and worse. They will scream property rights and freedom with billionaire megaphones, political contributions, and resistance, resistance to mandated reductions in fossil emissions and renewable replacements. It can't be done, their studies will prove, and even if it could be done, we couldn't afford it, and we don't need to since we've paid the same guys who said tobacco doesn't cause cancer and more to swear and prove that doubling and tripling carbon in the atmosphere doesn't change the global climate, and in effect, is good by making plants grow faster.

Sam Morrison: Focusing on carbon as Phil's key measure, and paying requisite attention to methane, forestry, and agriculture, the global challenge is vaguely analogous to the question of nuclear weapons. Since the bombing of Hiroshima and Nagasaki, many nations of all sorts have developed, stockpiled, and deployed nuclear weapons. They have been tested, but they have not been used. Even a state like the family-run totalitarianism of North Korea has not. The inhibitions on the mass emissions of carbon dioxide and greenhouse gases must face the same kind of inhibitions of use as do nuclear weapons.

Phil Clark: But of course, running a coal plant to make profits is not the same as dropping a bomb.

Wang Li: But the long-term consequences of continued mass fossil fuel combustion and pouring carbon dioxide into the atmosphere above twenty-one gigatons a year are similarly or more catastrophic than general nuclear war.

Phil Clark: Agreed. Use it by removing the carbon first, or capturing it before release, or leave it in the ground.

Pentti Aalto: The problem is getting all to practice this restraint before it is too late to make a real difference and we are at the mercy of the climate consequences we have unleashed. It's important to understand that the market is already driving decarbonization by the plunging costs of renewables and natural gas compared to coal. And it's hard to imagine that carbon capture and storage (CCS) plans would be cost effective compared with continuing decreases in cost of renewables that have, of course, zero fuel cost.

Phil Clark: But this isn't a debate about the viability and desirability of coal and oil as energy sources. Let's take it at a given, for now, that we have to use it cleanly and keep global carbon beneath three tons per person per year, or leave it in the ground. And that's not also considering all the other ecological consequences of fossil fuel use.

Ruth Johnson: We are well aware of the political, economic, and social power exerted by the oil patch and coal country, and the utilities that own the power plants that burn the coal or natural gas and emit the carbon. That infrastructure is the largest global agglomeration of capital. They see the value of their fuel reserves and their power plants to generate ongoing streams of profits. And that they are fighting tooth and nail to protect those profits and their investments from becoming "stranded."

Phil Clark: As global carbon dioxide levels rise and the ice melts.

Pentti Aalto: But we need to remember that ultimately the battle will be probably decided not by shutting down the existing plants en masse, but by not replacing the old ones with new ones, and by investment instead in the efficient renewable infrastructure. That's what we have to fight for. No more new fossil polluters.

Ruth Johnson: No more. Right now. No more. Three tons per person per year or bust. I think 350.org made a mistake when they made 350 parts per million the global goal without including the three tons of personal emissions per person per year the individual and national target. It tells you clearly as a person, as a community, how you are doing in comparison with others and how close or how far away you are from the goal.

Bob Irving: It says something to me if I build a net 1.0 tons carbon per person per year subdivision. I build my subdivision, as I know how to do, with affordable super-insulated and ultra-low infiltration houses that are easily heated and cooled with a small split-system air source heat pump that takes energy from the air and is powered, as are the LED lights and high efficiency appliances, by a community photovoltaic array and a field of vertical axis wind turbines. The solar and wind also charges our electric vehicle batteries, and power wall storage batteries that also can, as needed, feed power into houses and into the electric grid during peak times when we can be a net exporter of energy. The community organic garden is also includes year-round greenhouse food production and is fertilized from organic waste from tilapia raised for protein. As we go on, the community has a 3-D printing center where much of what we need is fabricated from renewable inputs.

Phil Clark: 3-D printing is rapidly making enormous strides. They've now shown you can print human organs and body parts—from human arteries to organs like hearts and lungs and maybe even brains. The printer lays down layers of organic material and reproduces the structure of the original body part. I saw a human ear in a Petri dish that if it replaced your outer ear, it could circularize and function normally.

Bob Irving: This sounds like the Woody Allen movie where all that survived was the supreme leader's nose.

Phil Clark: Yes, it does. But it's true. Maybe coming soon to a supermarket near you. And the potential is also to "print" any food you desire like on Star Trek. Right now, they're using a biocompatible polymer to design and soon be able to print customized stents for coronary arteries.

Pentti Aalto: And your greenhouse and aquaculture and fab centers can, of course become enterprises, not just exercises in self-sufficiency.

Bob Irving: They could.

Phil Clark: But those goals of below three tons of carbon per person per year as well as reducing existing atmospheric carbon levels through sequestration in soil and biomass and more cannot be reached as a matter of individual effort, no matter how commendable and useful an example can be reproduced and pursued by a neighborhood, a city, a state, a nation, a hemisphere, a world.

Sam Morrison: Hence the relevance of the Green Republic and our discussions.

Ruth Johnson: Of course, all this technical stuff are details, a fog of details hiding the real questions of decisions about how we live now and in the future.

Bob Irving: Missing the forest while examining the trees.

13. Two Basic Assumptions for a Green Republic

Ruth Johnson: It's substantially useful to clarify three basic assumptions that encompass and recognize the possibility of both success and of failure. We've thrown around lots of numbers about carbon dioxide and energy. I want to be clear here without the numbers.

Bob Irving: Thank you. Clear my head.

Ruth Johnson: First, the practice of ecological sustainability is absolutely essential to escape from ecological catastrophe and global collapse of our civilization. Practices leading to global cooling must replace practices leading to global warming to keep it simple. Understanding, for sure, that there's more to global ecological health than avoiding climate catastrophe. But that's the *sine qua non* for saving ourselves. Second, we are considering a Green Republic as the means. We are accepting political democracy employed in some fashion as way to balance the forces of freedom and community to help achieve and maintain both a healthy political and ecological order. This is a way. Not the only way. Third, we are accepting markets employed in some fashion as the means for sustainable economic growth and conduct.

Bob Irving: Another piece of good news. The coffee and the Danish, coffee cake, and rugelach have arrived. No scones. I'll take the Danish and I object. Isn't sustainable economic growth an oxymoron. Don't we need to shrink to survive?

Sam Morrison: Wait, before we get way ahead of ourselves. Let me just note that the problem is the nature and the ecological consequences of economic growth, as well as the economic consequences. Confusing the ecological consequences of economic growth, which is what matters most, with the monetary profit or loss is a philosophical category error.

Bob Irving: How so?

Sam Morrison: If we replace all coal plants with solar electricity, it would mean trillions of dollars in productive and profitable investment and the creation of millions of sustainable jobs and an enormous decrease in pollution, depletion, and ecological damage. We can have enormous monetary growth that at the same time leads to enormous reduction in pollution and our ecological footprint.

Bob Irving: So I can build my net-zero energy houses from sustainable materials, make some bucks, and sleep soundly.

Sam Morrison: Yes, in principle, yes.

Pentti Aalto: So we have a common understanding. We are crafting principles for a Green Republic that's rooted first in ecological sustainability, and second using political democracy, third in markets of some sort. Of course, that does not address the question of social justice that's rooted in questions of power, choice, and efficacy.

Bob Irving: Who gets to be in control of their lives?

Sam Morrison: Yes, we cannot wish away or pretend that the response to emerging ecological catastrophe must not be dealt with directly, immediately, and powerfully, and that must be anchored in questions of social justice as a key expression of democracy. We are going to approach this from the standpoint of a Green Republic that can exist with many diverse variations. The longer we fail to act effectively to make economic growth mean ecological improvement, the more likely it is that necessity will mandate the imposition of a state of emergency imposed, at best, by a benign technocracy that will mandate and impose its rules and regulations.

Pentti Aalto: Yes. I have seen the future and it doesn't work. Survival on an unsurvivable planet is like the visions of surviving underground after nuclear war with General Buck Turgeson from Dr. Strangelove saying, "We must not allow a mine shaft gap!"

Bob Irving: Love that movie. "Gentlemen, you cannot fight here. This is the War Room!"

Pentti Aalto: Yes, in the Strangelovian vein, we can build underground cities in the high arctic if climate change accelerates. Underground to protect from an unfriendly environment where the climate might not be survivable. Underground where the distance from collapsing civilization would also form a barrier from desperate starving masses. Perhaps, the survivors in tens or hundreds of thousands, even millions, living fully underground. Entrances hermetically sealed for security. Anything needed produced or chemically extracted underground. Food grown using full spectrum LED lights, energy from renewable power for the fully underground structures using geothermal bore holes for energy. Perhaps the underground civilization would survive the great dying and persist for thousands of years as the ecosphere slowly recovered. Perhaps.

Sam Morrison: When my dad's friend Dina Abelson was a slave laborer at Auschwitz for one thousand nights, her barracks at the slave labor camp outside the extermination center, she was forced to work at an underground munitions plant. Dina did her best to try to make sure the ammunition would blow up when the Nazis pulled the trigger. The entrance to the factory was a through a door cut into a huge old dead tree that led to a ladder leading underground. That's the kind of future in store for us if we do not act for sustainability.

Phil Clark: Perhaps this surviving fraction of humanity underground will be reduced eventually to slaves by ruling robots. Technocratic robots deciding that it was much more efficient to reduce space and energy for food production, water, and waste attendant with people.

Bob Irving: Let's not go down some variation of supposed rational perfection in the Venus project rabbit hole. What I understand is to keep it straightforward. We must halt and reverse the march toward ecological self-destruction and be ecologically sustainable in the long run. Along with sustainability, we are accepting the principles of markets and of democracy in some form.

14. An Ecological Imperative

Sam Morrison: The imperative for the pursuit of ecological sustainability is a principle that must be followed by everyone, and by our Green Republic. It's what's called a categorical imperative. This is Kant in *Groundwork of the Metaphysics of Morals*.

Ruth Johnson: Of course, the problem is that everyone may not accept or agree with the categorical imperative, truth or logic or morality supporting it or not.

Bob Irving: That's why we have laws and regulations and cops.

Sam Morrison: That's part of the central issue for the Green Republic. We can accept and recognize a categorical imperative for ecological conduct conditioned by the pursuit of social and ecological justice, but there must be a structure of social power that manifests this beyond nodding in agreement. As we have seen that as Berlin noted, your freedom to swing your fist ends at my nose, and my freedom also means freedom from fear of your abuse.

Phil Clark: We have been more than willing to violate this principle of ecological and just conduct. Violate it not just because we didn't understand it, or didn't understand how to apply it, but just didn't care. We cared more about short-term profit than long-term survival and prosperity. We'd kill the last whale to make a buck, or cut the last tree, or drill the last oil well.

Sam Morrison: Again, the need for a Green Republic, to establish a framework for the polity and its law that makes the pursuit of sustainability the essential principle to support life, liberty, justice, and the pursuit of happiness.

Bob Irving: Aren't we assuming too easily that we need a Green Republic? Why not no government? Just self-management and voluntary associations. No police, no taxes, no army. Voluntary all of it.

Sam Morrison: The enormous ecological consequences for all people and all living beings call for a system of limitation to equilibrate conduct to ensure that it is sustainable. This means a system of market rules and political rules that focus the consequences of all our actions on maintaining sustainable ends in a global system with many billions of people.

Pentti Aalto: Enforced by the Green storm troopers.

Ruth Johnson: No. That's why I want us to embrace democracy, freedom, and community and self-management as central to the Green Republic. I want to maximize local initiative and minimize imposition of outside power.

Sam Morrison: That's called subsidiarity. That local groups have maximum say in issues that most directly affect them within the context of basic norms. There's a continuum from a hierarchical unitary single-party state on one end with zero freedom outside of hierarchical order, and, on the other end of the continuum, individual anarchism with little organization, no state, no law, and with maximum personal license and maximum personal choice.

Pentti Aalto: Why not keep it simple. There is no way to freedom. Freedom is the way.

Sam Morrison: There's no reason to believe that freedom without any constraint, freedom without community, will not just continue the march toward self-destruction.

Ruth Johnson: We are informed by Jeffersonian inclination that the government that governs best, governs least. To this we add explicit principles of self-management and local control, increase of social and economic relationships, support for personal and community participation by people in ownership of where they work, where they live, where they get food and water, where they go to school. Democracy must be expressed by more than an individual ballot choice, and the principle of one person, one vote can pervade the economic and social realms through ownership participation.

Pentti Aalto: Similarly, we are informed by von Mises's fear of the state and the countervailing power from free markets that we must respect, and the freedom from the imposition of the social planners and architects to reshape people's lives who were not either considered at all, or summarily ignored.

Phil Clark: There's also a well-founded fear in the imposition of plans by technocratic optimizers and managers imposing their grand plans and stepping on communities. It obliterated the Chicano communities around Chavez Ravine to build Dodger Stadium. It's building Brasilia in the jungle. It's Robert Moses master builder in New York bulldozing communities. It's the edifice complex of Albany erecting monuments to ego. It's the grand buildings of Washington DC tooth by jowl with extreme poverty and the homeless sleeping on heating grates.

Ruth Johnson: We should also remember that Jefferson's limited government made firm constitutional and legal provision for his wealth by owning slaves who worked the plantation of the man who wrote the Declaration of Independence—"that all men are created equal, that they are endowed by their Creator with certain unalienable Rights, that among these are Life, Liberty and the pursuit of Happiness. That to secure these rights, Governments are instituted among Men, deriving their just powers from the consent of the governed." Women, slaves, indentured servants, Native Americans, and men without property did not seem to be able to effectively claim these unalienable rights.

Phil Clark: No, they didn't. It's interesting to note that the Declaration includes a long bill of particulars of injuries and usurpations by the King against the colonies that concludes:

"He has excited domestic insurrections amongst us, and has endeavoured to bring on the inhabitants of our frontiers, the merciless Indian Savages, whose known rule of warfare, is an undistinguished destruction of all ages, sexes and conditions."

The domestic insurrections referred to are slave revolts. The Virginia Governor Lord Dunsmore offered enslaved people freedom in November 1775 if they would join the British Army. The racist rant against Native Americans was in response to their increasing resistance to westward expansion by colonists seizing their lands. Jefferson and Washington were both wealthy planation slaveholders who favored western expansion. Washington was surveyor and land speculator west of the Appalachian Mountains.

Ruth Johnson: Enslavement and genocidal land theft were the two-headed original sins of American freedom.

Wang Li: We need to be mindful of the contradictions been reality and aspiration, between liberty for white men of property and the universal practice of freedom and community and ecological sustainability.

Ruth Johnson: I agree we must neither be blind to reality or the limitations of the emergent original American republic, or in the emergent Green Republic we aspire to craft and inform with our best understanding.

Sam Morrison: It's the broadening and balancing of the practices of freedom and community that offers a path ahead. It's this building of personal, family, and community equity in all aspects of life that helps establish strong community countervailing forces against the imposition of illegitimate authority, whether governmental or corporate. It's another category error to simply identify illegitimate authority with the state and ignore the imposition of corporate power.

Pentti Aalto: If the poor residents of housing projects were the owners, had equity, there would be a vastly different dynamic than as confinement zones for the poor.

Phil Clark: Yes. The power wielded by a global corporation—an Exxon or a Monsanto—is quite different from the power of the local mom-and-pop grocery store. The more economic power and assets that are in the hands of all citizens, the more resilience from imposition of illegitimate authority. Not that this alone stops the powerful from destroying whole neighborhoods when the stakes are high enough, or poisoning the water supply in Flint, Michigan to save some bucks because they could.

Sam Morrison: The concern over the imposition of power, if the practical definition of law is obey the rich, is well founded. As is the understanding of José Arizmendiarrieta of the Mondragon cooperatives of the Basque region of Spain, who concluded that law can be the tool for the protection of the poor and powerless. It is the collective economic and political power of the cooperatives and their rules that stood against the imposition of power from both without and from within the cooperatives.

Bob Irving: Arizmendiarrieta?

Ruth Johnson: José María Arizmendiarrieta was a Basque priest steeped in progressive Catholic social doctrine who arrived at the right place at the right time, the industrial mountain city of Mondragon—Arrasate in Basque—just at the time when the tired Franco dictatorship turned things over to those wanting to develop markets in the 1960s. Working with smart engineering students—his students—he founded the first cooperative factory, Fagor, to make kitchen appliances. The cooperatives went from there to develop co-op schools, housing, factories, and, crucially, a cooperative bank, the Caja Laboral Popular, and its entrepreneurial division, to help organize and mentor new cooperatives. A great success story. An example of what can be done. But not a cookie-cutter model for universal duplication and our Green Republic.

Sam Morrison: For now, we can see that of first importance is the ongoing and successful pursuit of sustainability for any social system. Second, we need to address how a Green Republic conducts its actions in markets, politics, law, and philosophy to achieve the first principle of ecological sustainability. How it does it distinguish and rank what is sustainable from what is not? Over what time frame are these considerations undertaken? How does it conduct economic and political operations to achieve and maintain ecological ends? And how is all this done within the context of maintaining the balance between freedom and community, to minimize the imposition of illegitimate authority and maintain a prosperous, sustainable, and just social order?

Phil Clark: And now you're telling me that a sustainable social order is somehow just?

Sam Morrison: What I am saying is that the Green Republic is built for both sustainability and for justice. It is justice, the maintenance of the balance between freedom and community, that mitigates against the imposition of pollution and ecological damage by the rich and powerful against the poor and powerless. Balancing freedom and community is what, in reality, puts meat on the bones of justice as fairness. Justice is explicitly not just a matter of rights, but of responsibilities that come with these rights. The community law mitigates against polluting conduct by the poor as well as the rich to erect, protect, and maintain a framework of social and ecological justice. In this sense, the Green Republic is, and must be, an instrument for justice as well as ecological survival.

Pentti Aalto: Ecological justice is not merely a moral point, it's a social expression of biological reality, of the fundamental dynamics of the ecosphere of sustainability as a renewing process of the biosphere's ultimately healing response to all influences. This is manifest in a democratic social system balancing rights and responsibilities for all.

Bob Irving: That's interesting. Descriptive but not all that practical. What does that mean in the workaday world? How do we balance freedom and community and pursue sustainability in the context of social and ecological justice that means something beyond abstract word salad?

Pentti Aalto: Sounds good. I think I know maybe what that means, but...

Phil Clark: Provisionally, I'll accept as a first principle for the everyday pursuit of sustainability and social and ecological justice for a Green Republic as Getting Prices Right. What's sustainable must be cheaper. What is ecologically harmful must be very expensive. Sustainable goods and services must be cheaper, gain market share, and become more profitable. That's the everyday structure beyond thou-shalt-not laws, rules and regs to enforce sustainability.

Bob Irving: When I'm building a net-zero energy house, my decisions are driven by price and ecological effect. Obviously, if sustainable products were cheaper then polluting choices, that's what I'd buy. They'd gain market share, become more profitable, and attract more investment.

Pentti Aalto: Prices, above all, are what drive markets. Get the prices right, and markets will quickly lead to enormous changes. And by monetizing ecological value through Sustainability Credits, the financial and business systems become tools for ecological improvement. Prices as a tool for justice?

Sam Morrison: Government can set the market rules for getting price right. Government can set the standards for materials, for efficiency, for sustainability, for ecological consumption cycles based on zero pollution and zero waste.

Pentti Aalto: Every output becomes input to another process.

Bob Irving: Getting the prices right reinforces the efficacy and power of ecological standards.

Ruth Johnson: It's strange that discussing an ecological future leads us to a consideration not just of renewable energy and ecological production, but into engagement with prices, that aspires to employ profits as a tool to make the maximization of finance capital also a means for the regeneration of natural capital.

Pentti Aalto: That means, my friend, that we must absolutely get the prices right.

15. Prices as an
Ecological Tool

Sam Morrison: It must seem almost sacrilegious to some people to talk about the nature and structure of a Green Republic and consider questions of assessments, taxes, price signals.

Phil Clark: You'd have thought the injunction "do no ecological harm" would have been enough. End of story.

Pentti Aalto: Unfortunately not. Ecologically sound market prices are designed to internalize true costs of production and use in all goods and services.

Wang Li: Getting prices right sends clear signals up and down supply chains from raw materials to production to consumption to recycling, reuse, remanufacture, or disposal. Getting prices right means to an extent that it becomes easier for businesses to focus on maximization of profits, a la Milton Friedman, since this internalizes externalities and can include payment in support of social and ecological justice.

Bob Irving: So in this Green Republic as our sort of capitalist nirvana, more like Samuel Butler's Erewhon, or nowhere, you are suggesting we do what we want based on the confidence that price comes first and leads reliably to good conduct.

Phil Clark: Not really. Prices help direct and ease the way. But combining, first, legal mandates for ecological conduct and legal mandates for pursuit of social and ecological justice within context of rights and responsibilities, with, second, tax and fiscal measures to get prices right based on ecological impact and social justice, and with, third, Sustainability Credits to make it extremely profitable for businesses to pursue carbon dioxide displacement and eventually all sorts of ecological measures. Together, these three measures form a structure that balances on multiple levels freedom and community by applying broad mandates of rights and responsibilities.

Pentti Aalto: So, for example, baked into the corporate profit pie are clear price signals set by ecological taxation to encourage sustainability, as well as strong incentives from Sustainability Credits, and a back-end tax structure, if needed, to support social and ecological justice and measures like a living wage and/or basic income grant.

Wang Li: This is a world in some aspects that would be different, but not completely unfamiliar to existing corporados and banksters, where investment and purchasing decisions and business plans are shaped by clear prices, tax signals, and regulatory signals.

Bob Irving: Yes. The point being in this Green Republic, nothing gets thrown away and no one gets thrown under the bus.

Sam Morrison: My dad once found a plastic supermarket food tray in the woods, discarded from someone's shopping. The plastic was embossed with the WR Grace logo. He, I think, mailed the tray back to the company with a note calling for proper disposal or recycling or reuse.

Pentti Aalto: Almost nothing we produce in a sustainable order gets tossed. The thought that materials once sold are no longer the responsibility of the producer is an artifact of a one-way high-waste high-pollution production regime. While sustainable production is essentially a circular economy where what is sold is eventually collected to be reused, remanufactured, recycled.

Wang Li: Like the good cheap restaurant, nothing is wasted. Right now, most global production cycles are the shipment of raw materials to China who manufactures products as a global factory and ships the products back to where they largely become waste.

Pentti Aalto: Circular ecological production would allow none of the manufactured materials to enter the waste stream. Instead, all production would be designed to facilitate reuse, remanufacture, and recycling. Most organics are composted. Some digested or thermally gasified for energy production.

Sam Morrison: Getting the prices right can happen in two ways. First, by assessments paid on polluting, depleting, or ecologically destructive products. Second, by subsidies on sustainable products.

Pentti Aalto: Energy is a good example. Fossil fuels in general are allowed to freely pollute up to approved emission levels. In addition to a free ride for approved pollution, they also receive a variety of subsidies and tax credits. Solar electric systems are quickly decreasing in price as well as increasing in efficiency and rapidly gaining market share. At the same time, they have also been the recipient of a variety of support mechanisms such as tax credits, purchase subsidies through feed-in tariff long-term contracts at sufficient prices, and the creation of Sustainability Credits, a regulatory asset created through carbon displacement and monetized for further investment.

Sam Morrison: But we need to remember we don't necessarily have to get the prices right all the time. We can just simply mandate an increasing percentage of renewables, and we will build what we need instead of raising prices on fossil fuels or decreasing prices on renewables.

Pentti Aalto: Right. That's the renewable portfolio standard. We don't need a carbon tax or a gas tax. We just need to mandate an ever-increasing percentage of renewables. That can be supported by a long-term feed-in tariff that's market bid driven to keep prices at the lowest level to pay for the renewables. They have zero fuel cost, and what we need to pay for is the capital cost and small maintenance costs.

Phil Clark: That's the price system working in terms of optimizing cost of renewables, but not by raising the price of poison power which is simply legislatively limited.

Bob Irving: That's the key part that government can play in the ecological turn in setting market rules that mandate change that needs to happen and a timetable to support it.

Pentti Aalto: That's the simplest, most economical and most straightforward way from here to there. It's not an aspiration of 50 percent renewables or 75 percent renewables or 100 percent renewables by some future date. It's a firm commitment with a mechanism to make it happen. It means, in practice, no more coal plants and natural gas plants, beyond some transitional natural gas plants that might be needed if battery technology and decentralized renewables aren't good enough quickly enough.

Phil Clark: I think whenever we leave any fossil fuel wiggle room, they'll worm their way through it.

Bob Irving: The only wiggle room is if we really try and we can't make it happen to meet the schedule.

Pentti Aalto: The schedule can be aggressive, but not too aggressive. And problems may arise, say in going from 75 percent to 100 percent renewables that weren't clear.

Phil Clark: But that's an optimization question. And we might have already met and then surpassed our three tons of carbon per person per year target, cut back methane, wring carbon from the air into soil and forests. Game over. Game won.

Sam Morrison: Yes, if we were really serious about saving ourselves and our civilization, it would be a back-planning exercise. Here's the binding goal. Here's how we reach that goal planning from now to then, and revisiting and revising that planning as we go to stay on track.

Pentti Aalto: If we were serious.

Wang Li: If we were.

Phil Clark: Wait a minute. Are we dumping price for something else?

Sam Morrison: I don't think we're dumping price, but we are entertaining the potential for alternative regimes that need not involve basic ecological tax reform that we want to examine for the Green Republic. It can work to meet important parts of tasks to help save our asses before too much carbon leads irreversibly to catastrophic ecological problems.

16. ALTERNATIVE REGIMES FOR QUICK RESPONSE

Phil Clark: We shouldn't underestimate the role and importance of government in establishing market rules, regulations, and laws that can lead to quick and decisive action.

Pentti Aalto: The classic has been the Montreal Protocol in response to the destruction of the protective ozone layer by escaping chlorofluorocarbon refrigerants in the upper atmosphere. CFCs were regarded as perfect replacements for ammonia-based refrigeration. CFCs were nontoxic, stable, easy to use, and well suited for refrigeration and air conditioning. Unfortunately, they reacted in the upper atmosphere with ozone that protects the earth's surface from the harmful effects of UV rays. They are also powerful greenhouse gases.

Wang Li: The Montreal Protocol established a plan to phase out CFCs and replace them with other refrigerants much less harmful to ozone and phase them in over time. As a global matter, government led industry in a process of banishing CFCs and rolling out replacements.

Pentti Aalto: The renewable portfolio standard can establish a plan to replace all energy with renewable substitutes in accord with an achievable ASAP time frame with investment capital easily supported by Sustainability Credits.

Bob Irving: But not too gradual.

Pentti Aalto: Agreed, not too gradual. Start at 2 percent a year and ramp up quickly to 5 percent to 10 percent a year. The feedback is from how we are doing on how many tons of carbon person per year we're emitting and how much sequestering, and if the global parts per million of carbon dioxide in the atmospheric rises or falls and by how much.

Phil Clark: Those scores on local and national tons of carbon per person per year and atmospheric concentration of carbon dioxide should be what we care most about, not the GDP, unless and until the GDP accurately reflects and accounts for increases or decreases in natural capital and not just a blind measure of finance capital.

Pentti Aalto: Call that the RNP, the Real National Product for an accurate account of the state of the world.

Sam Morrison: I agree.

Phil Clark: Remember, the renewable portfolio standard does not require taxation. It merely says the percentage of renewables must increase yearly. ASAP, fossil fuels have to be used without pollution or left in the ground.

Sam Morrison: The provision of renewable services can be based on a feed-in tariff model, where producers bid on what prices they can contract for to provide renewable power.

Bob Irving: The point is that efficient renewables eventually will provide all our energy needs. It's simply a matter of installing and networking renewables to heat and cool and light our homes, and power our vehicles and our factories.

Pentti Aalto: Efficiency, particularly second law of thermodynamic efficiency, can help allow a fivefold to tenfold increase of real efficiency—the energy in compared to useful work out. That's made possible by such tools as heat pumps and the Carnot cycle for cooling and refrigeration.

Ruth Johnson: There's no way you can make the Carnot cycle sexy. But we can understand we can improve efficiency as part and parcel of the life of the Green Republic by 500 percent to 1000 percent in many of our activities.

Pentti Aalto: Good engineering and material science.

Wang Li: A Green Republic must be more than a collection of efficient renewable technology or a civilization optimized by engineers.

Phil Clark: Like the Venus project.

Wang Li: Again, efficient renewable technologies are a necessary, but not sufficient, expression of a Green Republic. What's central is to make the social choices that create and use efficient renewables and the whole panoply of sustainable ways of life in all its aspects.

Sam Morrison: Yes, given a global high technology civilization with several billions of inhabitants, there's no other choice to achieve sustainability than to adopt comprehensive techniques and methods that preserve, protect, and nurture natural capital.

17. Justice, Justice, Back to Justice

Ruth Johnson: Now there's the Marxian view that technology potentiated the form of social organization—the grinding wheel gave us feudalism; the steam engine, industrial capitalism; and perhaps, the computer and the photovoltaic cell will lead to an ecological social order.

Wang Li: For comrade Marx, class struggle was integral to change and social evolution. The motive force.

Bob Irving: The fight between the rulers and the rules, between bosses and workers, wolves and rabbits.

Phil Clark: And now the fight between the polluters and the ecologists.

Sam Morrison: But, in reality, wolves and rabbits were interdependent—the health of one crucial for the health of the other maintained durable balance.

Wang Li: Here's where Marx's struggle paradigm for social and biologic evolution separates. Our survival and the health of the ecosphere is now dependent upon the provision of mutual aid and coevolutionary steps for regeneration of natural capital.

Pentti Aalto: Unquestionably, we are at the cusp of moving from a high-pollution, high-waste and, therefore, inherently self-destructive industrial order, toward a low-pollution, low-waste sustainable order.

Sam Morrison: An interesting question for us is the dynamic between the polluting bosses and rising green industry, between

Exxon and Peabody coal and Google and Apple. Classically, the bosses would make common cause. But it's clear that the well-being of polluters means catastrophe for nonpolluters or smaller polluters like Google and Apple.

Pentti Aalto: Saving grace almost certainly will not be provided by the revolution of the green bosses. Information is the high profit center of the twenty-first century. But that doesn't mean that Microsoft or Google or Apple or Amazon is a force for liberation.

Bob Irving: You mean Tim Cook, Mark Zuckerberg, and Jeff Bezos will not save us.

Phil Clark: Not by themselves. And not without some gentle persuasion.

Sam Morrison: Central to the Green Republic is the democratic rising from below. The action based on one person, one vote and not one dollar, one vote.

Bob Irving: Yes, sustainability will be the consequence of fundamental and pervasive social transformation of all aspects of our civilization.

Wang Li: It cannot and will not be conferred upon us by green billionaires, like Elon Musk, who can make important contributions toward accelerating the process of sustainable technological change. But the world created by Elon Musk might not be much different from the world created by General Motors, and it is not a venue for social and ecological justice and pervasive healing change.

Pentti Aalto: Elon Musk is doing both good and well. But a Green Republic is neither reducible to, or arising from, corporate forms in ecological markets any more than green technology will mean a Green Republic.

Ruth Johnson: We are talking a nonviolent social revolution. A democratic one here.

Pentti Aalto: And one outfitted with all kinds of ecological market rules for profit seeking that means the increase of natural capital as well as finance capital manifest through the practice of social and ecological justice and operationalized and guided, in part, by a strict definition of fiduciary responsibility.

Bob Irving: That doesn't sound sexy. It may be true, but it doesn't sound sexy.

Ruth Johnson: We are not likely to hear people chanting, "New market rules now!"

Bob Irving: Maybe, "Sustainability now!"

Sam Morrison: Let's hope.

Phil Clark: The very existence of ecological markets depends on the adoption of new ecological market rules, standards, laws, and regulation, investments, and taxes and assessment policy. Durable healing change cannot simply arise from profit maximizing green businesses. The skeptic in me says, maybe.

Sam Morrison: Maybe what?

Phil Clark: Maybe we can build a strong enough and dynamic enough structure to domesticate the market and make it do our bidding and build enduring sustainable prosperity and an ecological civilization. Kind of a pipe dream? Yes? No?

Sam Morrison: I'd say not a pipe dream. Because we are talking about democratic social structures that are focused on ecological ends that provide clear paths for sustainable profit, mitigated and contained by ecological and social justice.

Ruth Johnson: Without social and ecological justice, the fundamental dynamics of the Age of Pollution will tend to persist. It is not the good intentions or good character of a Green Fortune 100 or 500 that will lead to ecological sustainability. Rather, the complex of market rules, laws, regulations, tax and investment policies, and valuing sustainability through Sustainability Credits that will channel and shape the Green Republic following and expanding upon Article One for ecological conduct. Key is making the pursuit of sustainability a central concern, supported by strong and broad democratic participation on all levels.

18. Inequality as Reality

Bob Irving: Yeah, I read that sixty-two billionaires are as wealthy as the poorest half of the world's population. That's 3.7 billion people. That means my calculator app says a ratio of sixty million to one in assets between the world's sixty-two richest to the 3.7 billion poorest. And globally, that means one percent of the population own more than the combined assets of the remaining 99 percent. That's the world we've created through industrial capitalism.

Phil Clark: Glancing through *The New York Times Magazine*, there's some very interesting ads for apartments in Manhattan and in Miami. You can live in the Carlton House at 21 East 61 St. and Madison starting at $7.95 million an apartment. Or, if you'd like a Hudson River view, you can move into a condo at One Riverside Park, four to seven bedrooms from $7.62 million to over $25 million. And fortunately for the cash-strapped tenants, we're told a twenty-year tax abatement is in effect.

Bob Irving: That's stunning. People who can pay $25 million dollars for an apartment won't have to pay their fair share of taxes to the city. This is the world made for the pleasure of the one tenth of one percent, the richest of the rich.

Phil Clark: And if you're a snow bird and want to spend your winters in Miami, you can go in style to the Ritz-Carlton residences and villas at Miami Beach from $2 to $40 million developed by Lion Heart Capital. For sale are 111 lakefront residences in a ten-story low-rise plus twenty-five villas on Surprise Lake. You can choose from 1,700 to 11,000 square feet of floorspace. Better hurry. It's reported to be now past the 65 percent sold milestone. "In the end, it is the Ritz-Carlton brand, and level of staff training, which will make the residents feel like they are coming home and not living in a hotel, that is resonating with our buyers." And for those on a budget, there's IRIS on the Bay three – and four-bedroom townhomes with boat slips, private elevators, and gated entry (of course) from $800,000 up.

Ruth Johnson: In these terms, social justice can scarcely be said to exist. In Miami-Dade County in 2019, 19 percent of the population of 2.6 million were living below the poverty level. This was in pre-pandemic times. There were also 23,328 homeless in Florida in 2020. And it should not be a surprise that given such disparities of wealth and power, and without social justice, there is not ecological justice. The masters make the rules and reap the rewards while the billions face the consequences.

Wang Li: And call it freedom. And we now have our billionaires in China, although we have lifted many millions from poverty. To a comfortably polluting upper-middle class.

Sam Morrison: I was once taken to an upscale restaurant in Beijing for lunch at Houhai Lake. Clearly it was China, but the people were uniformly fashionable in a high international style. The women elegant and beautiful. The men wearing fine suits and ties. Everyone's hair styles just so. It struck me that I could have been in New York or Paris or Tokyo or Mumbai.

Pentti Aalto: Everyone's dream is to join the party.

Wang Li: Yes, to sit in endless traffic jams and breathe clouds of toxic air where the skyscraper tops are invisible.

Sam Morrison: The first time my dad I went to Los Angeles in the early 1980s, he told me he walked out of a friend's house on the second day and suddenly saw the Santa Monica Mountains looming nearby. They had been completely shrouded by smog the day before, and he didn't know they were there.

Pentti Aalto: You can usually see them now after a few decades of emissions reductions. Yeah.

Wang Li: We all share of our version of the dream. The Chinese dream. The American dream. On and on.

Bob Irving: And of course we all want to raise the gangplank and stop the newcomers from coming on board. Since we all can't live that dream that would take five earths to fulfill.

Wang Li: But we only have one.

Phil Clark: One indeed.

Sam Morrison: My argument is that it's the complex structure of incentives and disincentives crafted and democratically maintained by the Green Republic that can and will govern the shape of sustainable things to come.

Phil Clark: So you think we can square the circle and make the market and technology perform by instituting and maintaining enough just so's that we will pull ourselves back from the edge of catastrophe and then have a durable and ongoing ecological civilization?

Wang Li: I agree with Sam that's it a sensible value proposition based on strong feedback loops that channels business onto sustainable paths moving toward ecological improvement, and crucially toward social and ecological justice. And it helps if we have real understandable measures to monitor our progress, like tons of carbon per person per year locally and nationally, and atmospheric concentrations of carbon globally, along with reports of the RNP (Real National Product), not just meaningless financial accounting of GDP that values oil spills the same as real productive action.

Bob Irving: It's not going to work to build an ecological civilization where the mass of impoverished and homeless find shelter under the arrays of solar collectors.

Sam Morrison: We're alleging that markets, democracy, and justice applied to the use of sustainable technologies in a Green Republic can make economic growth mean ecological improvement.

Ruth Johnson: That's four pillars supporting a social system that's clearly not a species of dictatorial technocracy.

Wang Li: What makes you think that the power of capital just won't overwhelm the kind attentions of democracy once again? Like Thomas Piketty writing on how capital has rolled back the social democratic institutions that build the middle classes and is transferring wealth and power upward. Hence the billionaires in command as never before.

Ruth Johnson: Because the prospect for salvation from a Green Republic is the nature of the system we are talking about. Democracy that's more than quadrennial presidential plebiscite for rulers, social and ecological justice that's supported by durable means for justice and fairness, and ecological conduct that shapes and conditions sustainable market activity.

Pentti Aalto: What makes me think it's possible from a market perspective is that, at the bottom, it means making the price system work. It means getting an accurate price. The price in an ecological market is based on real costs, eliminating externalities so producers, consumers, and investors are more reliably guided by real prices to make choices.

Ruth Johnson: And it means strong mechanisms like a negative income tax or basic income grant for all, as part of a global convergence on fair distribution of resources for all. That each person will have adequate resources, for good food, shelter, water, health care, education.

Pentti Aalto: It doesn't mean equality for all. It also can't mean the status quo world where 1 percent has more than 99 percent, or sixty-two billionaires have more than 3.7 billion poor.

Ruth Johnson: Unless we want to hypothesize a world of voluntarily beneficent billionaires and benign plutocrats.

Pentti Aalto: Of course, the Carnegies, the Fords, the Pillsburys eventually did good works with their fortunes. Just as Bill Gates and Warren Buffet are embarked on that path.

Sam Morrison: Philanthropy is indeed commendable and important. The deeply religious frequently tithe even if they are far from rich. But we cannot reliably count on the beneficence of the rich to cure the problems of fundamental inequalities and monumental disparities of wealth and power. Taxation is in general the social response to market failure, not charity.

Phil Clark: What the strong democracy of the Green Republic must be about is more than redistributive policies. It's very much about the creation of sustainable wealth from many trillions of dollars of productive investment in sustainability. To build the efficient renewable energy infrastructure, the industrial ecological system, the sustainable agriculture and aquaculture systems to make economic growth mean ecological improvement and the improvement and regeneration of natural capital. To this, you add government action to set the rules, avoid market failure when necessary, and get things right on an ongoing basis.

19. Investments in Sustainability

Bob Irving: This isn't about shrinking. It's about sustainable growth that leads to ecological improvement. And therefore, if this is to work, it's about enormous productive investments in sustainability, and the generation of profits and finance capital along with the regeneration of natural capital and the growth of social and ecological justice as a consequence and part of the process. That's what we need to cling to and focus on.

Sam Morrison: Yes. Let's talk about investment in photovoltaics to replace coal plants. If I invest one trillion dollars...

Bob Irving: You have a trillion dollars?

Sam Morrison: OK. If we, the collective we, invest one trillion dollars in PV—at this scale, let's say PV costs $1.50 per watt installed. It would probably be $1.00 a watt. But let's say $1.50 to be conservative. For each megawatt, we need to invest $1.5 million and use four to six acres of land. For one trillion bucks we can build 666,676 MW of PV. And to replace all the output of the 1,309 mW of US coal plants would take $1.73 trillion. Big number all at once, but only a $90 billion a year investment over twenty years. Of course, the goal should be ten years if at all possible, with $180 billion a year. With Sustainability Credits in place, the investment numbers are not a problem.

Pentti Aalto: Being serious to get the work done quickly is. Of course, you wouldn't do it exactly that way since you have no storage to deal with when sun doesn't shine.

Sam Morrison: Yes, in reality, we'd combine solar with wind and other renewables and green hydrogen for generators produced by solar powered electrolyzers. On a continental scale or regional scale, the mixture of sun and wind and tide and geothermal is self-balancing when wired together through HVDC power lines. And we would use cheap battery storage whose price is also dropping like a stone. As well as more and more distributed PV from PV windows, PV paint, PV road materials, new small vertical wind, et cetera, et cetera.

Pentti Aalto: The point here is that the renewable transformation is a productive investment. Not a cost. An investment that slashed pollution, depletion, and ecological damage. Fuel costs go to zero. We no longer have to fight wars for oil. A $90 billion to $180 billion annual investment here given the risk if we don't, and the rewards if we do, is a no brainer.

Bob Irving: That creates millions and millions of sustainable jobs and sustainable communities.

Sam Morrison: So in a sense, the Green Republic is sustainability as a business opportunity, and a security imperative compared to business as usual.

20. Markets from Both Sides

Pentti Aalto: I'm focusing on perfecting the markets and the power of choice and competition and getting the rules right. It's the opposite of the exercise of monopoly power and the obscure ultra-complex financial instrument like credit default swaps and variations ad nauseam that transformed risk reduction tools into speculative bets.

Bob Irving: Speculative instruments of mass destruction, said Warren Buffet. No one is going to make money in the long run in markets that no one clearly understands.

Phil Clark: Adam Smith understood this and about the power of monopoly. "People of the same trade seldom meet together, even for merriment and diversion, but the conversation ends in a conspiracy against the public, or in some contrivance to raise prices."

Pentti Aalto: Smith realistically saw the dynamics of markets. He understood, that "Our merchants and master-manufacturers complain much of the bad effects of high wages in raising the prices, and thereby lessening the sale of their goods both at home and abroad. They say nothing concerning the bad effects of high profits. They are silent with regard to the pernicious effects of their own gains. They complain only of those of other people."

Phil Clark: That's my point. Those circumstances are eternal.

Ruth Johnson: Understood. That's why if we are to have a chance, the institutions of the Green Republic must be built with an understanding of such dynamics and an ability to counter them on an ongoing basis.

Phil Clark: Like the repeal of Glass-Steagall tore down the wall between investment banks and commercial banks after the great depression and that, surprise, led to the global financial collapse in 2007.

Ruth Johnson: I'm not arguing that there's no risk, and the task will not be ongoing. But institutions like chattel slavery once seemed dominant and eternal, or cannibalism for that matter. What was once central is now marginal.

Phil Clark: Replacing chattel slavery with wage slavery.

Ruth Johnson: Not the same.

Wang Li: And that's why there's a minimum wage. And now a living wage, since we didn't keep raising the minimum wage.

Sam Morrison: The problem is not a lack of techniques or methods. What we are about in a Green Republic is to codify the basis for long-term success.

Pentti Aalto: The advantage, such as it is, is that we are not trying to invent something completely new under the sun. But instead to adapt and, so to speak, engineer existing parts like democracy and markets and social justice into durable and sustainable forms. We're taking the nonpolluting high profit centers and generalizing and protecting them. We're not trying to cut the legs from under markets.

Phil Clark: That's what concerns me.

Bob Irving: Markets are no more evil than governments.

Ruth Johnson: What we're claiming in the Green Republic is that we can focus the realm of economic freedom on sustainable ends to support ecological community, and the realm of community to protect the realm of sustainable ecological market freedom and justice.

Wang Li: This is a somewhat more expansive version of Madison's view of checks and balances. That the realm of economic freedom, of life, liberty, property in action takes both an expansive understanding of life as the ecosphere, and that such action must be conditioned by sustainable conduct. And that the government and the community is, in large part, an expression

of the realm of political and economic freedom that must be protected and nurtured.

Bob Irving: Sort of too abstract for me. But I understand this
like a scale with two balance pans. One for freedom, the other community, and that the weight of each must balance.

Ruth Johnson: And that balance is the point of ecological sustainability and social and ecological justice.

Pentti Aalto: Adam Smith, by the way, had a very strong sense
of morality and social justice. His first major book was the *Theory
of Moral Sentiments.* That moral conduct and the opinions of others
mattered very much.

Wang Li: Yes, another tool in support of the Green Republic.
New wine in old bottles.

Bob Irving. Waste nothing. There's no "the expropriators have
been expropriated" Marxian blather and triumphalism.

Phil Clark: And also, no capitalism as end of history BS.

Pentti Aalto: Smith, by the way, was a strong opponent of slavery.

Phil Clark: Smith the moral philosopher died in 1790. He is
not necessarily to be blamed for lacking the vision of Blake of the
"dark satanic mills" of industrialism any more than Marx can be
held guilty for all the problems of Soviet Communism and all else
done in his name.

Wang Li: He did, after all, exclaim at one point, "I am not a
Marxist!"

Ruth Johnson: As I imagine Smith would have said, had he lived
longer, "I am not a capitalist," if he saw what was being defended
and advanced in his name.

Pentti Aalto: It's also interesting that Smith understood clearly
what Marx called surplus labor:

The value which the workmen add to the materials, therefore, resolves itself in this case into two parts, of which the
one pays their wages, the other the profits of the employer
upon the whole stock of materials and wages which he
advanced.

Sam Morrison: But we're not here debating the virtues and true beliefs of eighteenth and nineteenth century political economists. The Green Republic is a twenty-first century undertaking. And I think it's rooted in more than the historical cause-and-effect thinking. I think the Green Republic anchor will be understood as a complex and evolving system. A complex political ecosystem that exists in interrelationship with the ecosphere as a whole.

Phil Clark: Yes. It's the expression of emergent phenomena where conscious human behavior becomes a part of the fundamental process of sustainability and coevolution—where the planet shapes life and life shapes the planet. It's a complex, emergent, self-organizing, evolving, and interactive system to be judged by the health of social sphere and ecosphere, and their ongoing interactions.

Ruth Johnson: Let's break for dinner and then continue our discussion.

Phil Clark: Agreed.

All Agreed.

Bob Irving: Then let's do it.

21. Green Republic as Complex System

Bob Irving: Meagan, I wanted to know more about your bee adventures. First, was it a good trip back from the jungle, Meagan?

Meagan Simons: Once we took the boat from the island, it was a taxi driving too fast to the airport. Nonstop from Panama City in eight hours, after three months on Barro Colorado finding nests, at last, of the orchid bees.

Phil Clark: Good digs at the institute?

Meagan Simons: Comfortable enough. They cook mostly rice and beans. Air conditioning only in the lab. Bedrooms have good screens. So days are spent finding bee nests inside hollow rotten twigs in the jungle, collecting pupae, and then working on them in the lab.

Phil Clark: You're studying?

Meagan Simons: Orchid bees are interesting creatures. The males, not the females, are pollinators of orchids. They are gorgeous iridescent green bees where, as you watch them work, the males are scraping things, particularly from orchids. They're attracted by the fragrance.

Phil Clark: For food?

Meagan Simons: Not for food.

Phil Clark: Then for what?

Meagan Simons: That's what's interesting. The males scrape odiferous pollen from orchids and store it in pouches on their hind legs that they use to make strong pheromones to attract the females. I'm studying the nature of successful pheromones, and the factors that influence successful pheromone producers. Whether such success just favors the busy bee, or is it selection of particular species of orchids at particular times, or are successful bees just really good pheromone producers.

Bob Irving: I could see the commercial applications of that. Bee pheromone scent for men.

Pentti Aalto: It could be in everything from men's deodorant to shaving cream to toothpaste.

Bob Irving: Or a standalone stick.

Phil Clark: There's the market-based approach to the wonders of nature springing into action. And I suppose that under the International Convention on Biological Diversity, there will be benefit sharing for the local inhabitants.

Bob Irving: Yes. Probably tens of thousands for the locals.

Phil Clark: And millions for the corporados.

Bob Irving; Don't forget the money skimmed off the top by local government. It's expensive auditing these things.

Meagan Simons: As I understand it from Sam Morrison, we're here for something a little more grand than bee pheromones, the Green Republic.

Phil Clark: That's what they say.

Meagan Simons: I think there's value here in considering the Green Republic as a biosocial phenomenon. It's like our bee pheromone question writ large.

Phil Clark: Meaning?

Meagan Simons: Two things. First, right in our face is the question of the meaning of sustainability and of its connection to social and ecological justice.

Phil Clark: Yes, we have to add a dash of social justice and a tablespoon of ecological justice to bake the sustainability pie and get it just right.

Meagan Simons: More than that. I used to think social and ecological justice was just an add on. Like sustainability plus one, or sustainability prime. But after some years in the jungle and relating to the people living there and their struggle, I'm beginning to have a different opinion.

Phil Clark: What's that?

Meagan Simons: That social and ecological justice isn't an epiphenomenon of sustainability. We have it turned on its head. Sustainability as conscious practice is an expression of social and ecological justice.

Sam Morrison: The living world, pre-homo sapiens, handled itself quite well. Sustainability was an inherent coevolutionary expression of the biosphere. In response to all influences, life responded in ways that would help render conditions maximally favorable for life, for all life. This is what was evolutionarily selected. This is what reshaped the nature of the biosphere in response to catastrophic mass extinctions that wiped out a large percentage of species.

Phil Clark: But life recovered and healed and transformed the planet over time in ways maximally suitable for life in all its diversity.

Sam Morrison: Respective of no particular species or class or order.

Meagan Simons: The point we missed is that the ecosphere did quite well without us. Sustainability and its processes are fundamental characteristics of the ecosphere. In the twenty-first century, the conscious human practice of sustainability is the latest arrow in the quiver of the ecosphere. That human intervention is not simply the result of natural catastrophe, but in response human-induced changes of the Anthropocene that now have influence on a geophysical scale.

Sam Morrison: And therefore, it is the practice of ecological and social justice that represents the healing response to industrial excess that caused the ecological problem.

Phil Clark: It's not just a matter of a technological fix. Social and ecological justice means the amelioration and reversal of the conditions that caused the ecological problem.

Bob Irving: We're talking about conditions caused by humanity. Humanity must be the solution.

Ruth Johnson: There's also a fine dance between mitigation, meaning repair, and adaptation to the consequences of human action like climate change.

Pentti Aalto: Social and ecological justice cannot be limited to buying air conditioners for the poor to make heat waves more tolerable. This is adaptation without repair and mitigation. Without changing what's caused and causing the ecological crisis.

Phil Clark: Adaptation that, in fact, makes it worse. That's more a social Band-Aid than justice.

Sam Morrison: Social and ecological justice does not mean that the world is at the service of humanity. Instead, it's got to be the opposite. Humanity must be at the service of an afflicted planet, of an ecosphere afflicted by humanity. The well-being of humanity cannot be separated from the health and well-being of the ecosphere. We cannot have one without the other.

Phil Clark: And, of course, the greatest suffering is by the poor, and poor nations, who were not responsible in large measure for the ecological depredations in the interest of the rich and powerful.

Meagan Simons: It is the health of ecosystems as a whole, supported by the practices of social and geological justice, that is the expression of sustainability in action. The context of social and ecological justice plays out for individual people and particular communities that matter, as do individual species and particular places. Whose lives and whose homes matter are of course the fundamental social and political question of justice and what a Green Republic is supposed to be about—social and ecological justice for all.

Ruth Johnson: This isn't about the goodness of our hearts. It's a survival imperative for all of humanity, for sustainability, for the prospects for prosperity, for peace and justice.

Meagan Simons: And justice here encompasses Rawls's concept of justice as fairness. But it' s more than that. The pursuit of social and geological justice is the expression of both freedom and community in the dynamic pursuit of sustainability.

Sam Morrison: It's the pursuit of self-interest from the standpoint of both freedom and community that balances, undermines, and corrects excesses.

Wang Li: You're saying that sustainability is the ecosphere's countervailing response to excess, in our case through the medium of social action.

Sam Morrison: Yes, this social action is community action. It is undertaken by individuals in a community. It's a preeminently Aristotelian expression of humanity as a social animal making individual and social choices. Individual choices that are an expression of character and personal virtue. Social choices that are the balance point between freedom and community.

Meagan Simons: And that balance point is justice with its social and ecological manifestations.

Sam Morrison: Correct. Just as without freedom, community suffers, and without community, freedom suffers. And social and ecological justice are similarly interdependent.

Meagan Simons: And all together constituent a homeostatic system facilitated by democracy and constitutional order built around our Article One: The Ecological Imperative.

Wang Li: This represents the deep structure of sustainability. Elements that cannot be easily torn asunder, for if they are, the systems rapidly become unbalanced, unstable, and loses equilibrium and their ability for self-healing.

Phil Clark: Like we were, or are, in the pre-Green Republic era.

Sam Morrison: Yes. Subject to the effects of the practice of business and pollution as usual.

Phil Clark: The ecological crises is confirmation of the thesis that profit seeking at the expense of people and the ecosphere is not only unjust, but self-destructive.

Pentti Aalto: Now, how to pursue social and ecological justice is another question. There's the argument of the tragedy of the commons, that private property and private ownership, or state ownership and control, is the only way to pursue such justice which is otherwise ephemeral and futile.

Phil Clark: And there's another view based on maintaining the integrity of the commons through its self-management and effective self-regulation by local communities to protect it from the avaricious schemes of corporations and governments.

Sam Morrison: Yes, we must explore and understand both the paths the Green Republic can follow to reach and maintain social and ecological justice, and the tools to employ. But, before we lose track, I'd like to hear what was Meagan's second point about the Green Republic as biosocial phenomena.

Meagan Simons: OK. Going beyond sustainability as a biological imperative and social tool, are there particular dynamics of the ecosphere that can help inform and guide us, inform the nature, role, and conduct of a Green Republic for the long run?

Sam Morrison: Obviously, the ecosphere doesn't tell us if we should have a multiparty parliamentary style system, or a two-party presidential style system, or a monarchy.

Meagan Simons: The bees would tell us they favor the monarchy. But I'm not talking about selecting analogies that justify whatever we want to do. I'm suggesting that by understanding the operation of ecosystems we run ultimately into something deeper.

Sam Morrison: Meaning?

Meagan Simons: Meaning that when we look at ecosystems and their dynamics, we find a number of unusual things and tendencies. One of these is the recursive nature of similar patterns of the action of ecosystems on a level from the backyard pond to the planet.

Pentti Aalto: For example?

Meagan Simons: For example, ecosystems are like coastlines, or the Mandelbrot set that repeat the same patterns at whatever scale. Another is the action of ecosystems as more than the sum of its parts. Ecosystems function in a way that they are not just influenced from the bottom up, but they act as to transform themselves as a whole, in effect, from the top down.

Sam Morrison: This is what Robert Ulanowicz calls process ecology. Ecosystems as wholes operate in accordance with thermodynamic principles. The behavior of ecosystems can be modeled and understood as information flows and the activity of cybernetic feedback loops. Ecosystems are characterized by ensembles of mutualisms, of symbiotic relationships that drive adaptation and evolution.

Phil Clark: As a physicist, what's interesting is that Ulanowicz is very much against reductionism as the basis for understanding action. He advanced three basic principles. First, chance matters and may disrupt any system or process. Second, a process, through mediation or by influence of other processes, may be capable of influencing itself. Third, systems differ from one another based on their history that is reflected by their material configurations.

Pentti Aalto: This is a sort of ecological metaphysics, challenging not the laws of physics, but scientific reductionism. Process ecology looks at ecosystems and its behavior as a whole. Scientific reductionism understands the world through observing the interaction of smaller and smaller parts. And then drawing inferences about the behavior and nature of very large systems and processes.

Robert Irving: Like trying to describe the nature and social life of a city by sawdust found at a construction site.

Pentti Aalto: Exactly.

Phil Clark: It's not that Ulanowicz is saying disregard quantum mechanics. He's focusing on the emergence of new conditions from the unique history and interactions of ecosystems and their processes.

Meagan Simons: Our social and historic perspective has changed first from considering the earth as timeless, divinely given, and guided, and then to that of the ecosphere as hotel and store to be enjoyed and used by humanity determined by scientific rules and subject to the ministrations and power of human technologies, and now to a constantly changing living system capable of being fundamentally changed, for better or worse, by the consequences of human action.

22. Ecosystems and Being

Meagan Simons: The nature of ecosystems and our changing relationship with the planet should raise in our minds the question, what is the nature of being? If being is not timeless, and instead is ever contingent on connections and relationships, then the distinction between being and knowledge, between ontology and epistemology, fades away into phenomenology and the dynamics of systems, and our roles and experiences within them. We're part of the world. In it. Of it. Irreducibly.

Bob Irving: Deeper waters than I'm used to for a carpenter, Meagan. Meaning?

Meagan Simons: Bob, I couldn't begin to design one of your timber frames, let alone out put it together. What I'm claiming here on an abstract level, in philosopher talk, is that we can't abstract qualities from things in themselves. And what matters most is the reality of our experiences with them, our engagement that's real, sensuous, experienced, not abstracted. That ecosystems engage us. That we are part of them.

Phil Clark: This is a step away from the ability to invent and define all kinds of qualities and invest them with all kinds of meanings. It warms my physicist heart to root things in the material, the physical, the experiential, the phenomenological, the world as experienced—the world as the self, and the other—connected by experience.

Sam Morrison: The world as experienced is contrary to Plato's idealism and his allegory of the cave, a world of absolutes and poor manifestations. But it doesn't mean phenomenology as articulated by Husserl or Heidegger, the experience of being in itself. That's literally true, but what Sam and Meagan are suggesting is not just a matter of sense perception as reality, but that what we experience, with all its warts, is the reality, with all its complexity. And that complexity is the emergent reality of ecosystems that now encompass our social behavior.

Meagan Simons: Ecosystems are exquisitely complex, dynamic, and unique entities. Of this uniqueness, biologist Stewart Kauffman concludes, "History enters the universe when the space of the possible is much larger than the space of the actual."

Phil Clark: Meaning history is an expression of a series of unique nonrepeating events. Life is not reducible to a physicist's equations. Even mine. And also, not just reducible to the primacy of perception. It's closer to the phenomenology of Merleau-Ponty, where science offers, at best, a limited abstraction, "always both naive and at the same time dishonest," he wrote in *Phenomenology of Perception*. We don't have to express truth. Truth is the thing in itself that we need to experience.

Sam Morrison: I think Meagan is swimming in similar waters, eco-phenomenological waters, of David Abram and Merleau-Ponty of The Visible and the Invisible, but not the primal phenomenological pond. This is Abram writing of "the biosphere as it is experienced and lived from within by the intelligent body—by the attentive human animal who is entirely apart of the world that he, or she, experiences." We don't need to throw out all the science along with the pond water. Meagan's saying along with Ulanowicz, who, by the way, was a chemical engineer, that the exquisite complexity of ecosystems cannot be predicted or reduced to simple physical equations, but must be experienced and lived.

Bob Irving: So you're saying that Paris is about much more than street maps, concrete, bricks, and its architecture.

Sam Morrison: You got it. If suddenly Paris was destroyed, everything organic turned to soil, all the books and electronic records gone, what would be left would be brick and stone. And from that stone, what could we really say about the unique character of life in Paris? From a surviving sculpture of an unearthed Rodin, we'd be able to draw some inferences. We could certainly not have described or predicted the world and culture of Paris street singers and the wonder of Édith Piaf from the character of the stone.

Phil Clark: There's an approach needed beyond physics and chemistry to understand and appreciate the ecosphere's unique nature, significance, and action. Understanding, of course that our perceptions are an interpretation, by their nature limited and partial and at a remove. But one that doesn't deny their reality and enormous complexity and history or the engagement and sensuous and transcendent nature, that Abram describes of our living perceptions of them.

Meagan Simons: Exactly. There's something transcending, absorbing, and wonderful of being with the bees and toucans in the jungle.

Sam Morrison: And with the bullet ants, the chiggers, and the balls of ticks.

Meagan Simons: Not them. It's not Eden. But it is magical and compelling, as well as exquisitely complex on a scale we have not appreciated. It's this compelling experience, not just "we gotta do it"—understanding is what will make the Green Republic the locus for transcendent action, joining hands in alliance with the sensuous living world. The complexity of that living world that has evolved is breathtaking.

Pentti Aalto: If we only consider all proteins made of two hundred amino acids, there are twenty to the two hundredth power of such possible proteins. There are estimated to be ten to the eightieth power of particles in the universe. If all they did was make proteins of two hundred amino acids on the Planck time scale, it would take ten to the thirty-ninth times the lifetime of the universe to make all these proteins just once. The contingency behind that pond ecosystem, let alone the tropical jungle that defines its uniqueness, is stunning.

Phil Clark: In my physicist heart, I must admit that complex biological systems or social systems, clearly, are grossly nonrepeatable. And it suggests a tendency in the universe toward autocatalysis or self-organization that Stewart Kaufman and Ulanowicz embrace. This doesn't mean that we cannot make predictive statements about the nature and behavior of pond ecosystems.

Meagan Simons. It does not. The influence of the laws of thermodynamics and information theory certainly still apply, but they are only descriptive and partially predictive.

Phil Clark: Sure.

Meagan Simons: Ulanowicz goes further and suggests causal holes in space-time. I won't go there.

Ruth Johnson: And many say there's an inherent telos or trajectory toward communication, consciousness, self-consciousness. Is that chance or destiny?

Phil Clark: You can have trajectory, the expression of potential without inherent purpose. A design without a designer. But a design nevertheless.

Meagan Simons: And Darwin himself noted, regarding your physicist heart, that the function of the heart is to pump blood, and the heart came into existence in the universe for that purpose.

Phil Clark: And therefore, it's hard to show how the coming into existence of the heart on planet earth was entailed by the laws of physics, which are the same throughout the universe.

Meagan Simons: And we can't pre-state all possible Darwinian pre-adaptions or symbiotic possibilities, and mutual action selected for new evolutionary processes. Politically and socially, the dynamics of freedom and community are analogous to the behavior of ecospheres. We can't pre-state all potential political adaptations that might be relevant to the changing circumstances of a Green Republic.

Phil Clark: Nor can we pre-state the future conditions leading to evolutionary selection. And for that matter, our actions, biological actions influencing the planet, make changes in Earth's orbital dynamics, and thereby affect the universe—meaning also that the Green Republic can affect the universe.

Meagan Simons: Laws cannot sufficiently prescribe the evolution of the biosphere.

Phil Clark: Yes, laws are descriptive, not predictive, in evolutionary terms. We need not overturn the laws of physics, but we cannot reliably predict the future from existing conditions. And we cannot reliably predict emergent physical phenomena before they emerge from complexity, which immediately entails further response and further coevolution.

Pentti Aalto: Yes, the whole is very much more than the sum of its parts, and also the potential locus for the sudden emergence of entirely new things. That's the generative mystery of ecosystems in action including now their social manifestations.

Pentti Aalto: We need to wrap our minds around the biosocial nature now of evolution driving change on a geophysical scale.

Meagan Simons: It's sufficient for our purposes here to focus of the complexity of biosocial evolution. Human action is now changing the climate, altering fundamental patterns of the advance and retreat of ice on a planetary scale, creating a sixth planetary mass-extinction event.

Phil Clark: This is not small stuff.

Meagan Simons: And, to our point, humanity is now consciously practicing sustainability as a social doctrine that can have a healing planetary impact...

Bob Irving: We hope.

Ruth Johnson: And that's a coevolutionary leap. A socially emergent phenomenon that has potentially enormous biologic and geophysical consequences. That humanity can move from inadvertent or careless or deliberate ecological damage to reshape human behavior for the conduct of ecological healing and the health of the ecosphere and the achievement of human goals.

Sam Morrison: The Green Republic is a recognition of our roles as self-conscious stewards of the living world whose health and well-being is inextricably linked to ours.

Pentti Aalto: The Green Republic is fundamentally a recognition and the acceptance of the unavoidable role humanity must play as a global high technology civilization in the future health and well-being of the biosphere and therefore its evolutionary future.

Ruth Johnson: In that regard, it's extraordinary that globally, evolution is now fully entailed in self-conscious human action.

Meagan Simons: Evolution and physical consequences entailed in human self-consciousness.

Sam Morrison: Of course, so far, the self-destructive power of our behavior is much more powerful than our healing sustainable manifestations.

Pentti Aalto: Yes, conservation biology and economics need to become deeply acquainted in the Green Republic. Self-destructive conduct needs to become the exception and not the rule.

23. Making Article One Explicit

Bob Irving: One hopeful sign is the willingness of some large corporations to embrace sustainability concepts. GM and Toyota pursue zero-waste factories. Walmart, of all corporations, has strong sustainability practices in many areas like sustainable fisheries where they have enormous market power. Now Blackrock, the world's largest asset holder, is conditioning ownership of assets on companies reducing carbon dioxide emissions.

Phil Clark: They haven't heard the social justice message though.

Pentti Aalto: That's where the Green Republic makes explicit, following Article One, what must be done, and the market structures, rules, laws, and regulations to properly focus and reward action.

Sam Morrison: Yes. What's also central is the conduct for durable cybernetic feedback loops that must guide and equilibrate action in the Green Republic.

Phil Clark: Meaning?

Sam Morrison: Meaning that for the Green Republic to stay on course, it will need more than an organizational chart. There needs to be good information on consequences of action, and multiple pathways for feedback and democratic means to influence and adapt quickly to changing circumstances.

Ruth Johnson: Tools for social and ecological justice, tools for empowerment, participation, and strong democracy are not just extraneous filigrees, but central to the long-term success of the Green Republic.

Bob Irving: Are we finally getting off our high abstract horses and putting feet on the ground? It's kind of interesting when people want to talk about ecology and sustainability instead of talking about living things and the physical world surrounding us, weave great abstract webs.

Phil Clark: Yes, it is. So to sort of summarize what we've concluded from the complexity of ecosystems that now include the biosocial/physical component is that there's no real validity, no meaning at all, in attempting to separate ourselves from the living world. This biosocial/physical component is an emergent generative phenomenon manifested in the pursuit of sustainability whose now inescapable social component is the expression of social and ecological justice. We can't go back.

Pentti Aalto: We can practice eco-technology. We can make economic growth mean ecological improvement and the regeneration of ecosystems and natural capital. But we can't just apply seventeenth century technology in the twenty-first century in a world of more than eight billion people and expect to once again have seventeenth century ecological problems.

Phil Clark: We can and must dramatically change how we do things. For example, the US uses about seven billion barrels of crude oil a year. That's billion with a B. About three-quarters of that, when refined, was burned as gasoline (47 percent), heating oil and diesel fuel (21 percent), and jet fuel (8 percent). The rest of it as used as asphalt and as chemical feedstocks.

Pentti Aalto: The average barrel of crude yields about 220 pounds of liquid fuels that, when burned, each pound of fuel carbon combines with oxygen to yield 3.15 pounds of carbon dioxide. That means each barrel of crude, when refined and the fuels burned, produces 693 pounds of carbon dioxide. Totaling 2.425 billion tons of carbon per year. That's 7.5 tons per person per year for each of the 321 million Americans for our oil addiction.

Meagan Simons: And the sustainable global level for carbon is three tons per person per year globally. The pursuit of sustainability and social and ecological justice must mean replacing our oil, our coal, and natural gas with renewables, or use it without carbon release, or leave it in the ground.

Sam Morrison: That's the task for the Green Republic. To face the music while we are still able to dance. This means a technological transformation for efficient renewables that will mean enormous investment, and economic growth meaning dramatic ecological improvement. By the numbers.

Pentti Aalto: And we're back to putting our feet on the ground both figuratively and literally.

24. Property in the Green Republic

Sam Morrison: Yes. Let's touch on another important point to look at justice in the Green Republic—social and ecological justice from a slightly different direction—that of property.

Phil Clark: OK. Is there a particular property regime that is consonant with the health of the ecosphere and of the Green Republic? Or can we reach common ends through different means?

Pentti Aalto: Of course, we can start with the vulgar dichotomy advanced by both the right and by the left around private or social property. Depending on whatever side of the aisle you sit, one or the other is expression and even the source of all evil, of tyranny, exploitation, and abuse.

Phil Clark: Yes, private property is an expression of land of the commons enclosed and privatized by the lords. Private property is the instrument of serfdom, of the extraction of rents from the poor by the rich. Private property is the ownership of the factories and the commodities by the capitalist from which the surplus labor of workers is extracted to create wealth and more private property by the rich. Private property is the song of the plantation owner. Buy more land to grow more cotton to buy more slaves to buy more land…Ecological and social justice matters not one whit. Private property is to be enjoyed—that is, exploited—in the name of property rights. Where human rights or ecological rights do not enter into the equation. This is the realm of capitalist private property nirvana. Blessed by Milton Friedman's declaration that the pursuit of social good is to make more money for shareholders.

Pentti Aalto: Yes, and social property is the expropriated land and hard-earned wealth seized by the state, not just from the wealthy, but from everyone, from the farmer and the shopkeeper, to the builder, the craftsperson, the artisan scarcely able to keep their heads above water. Social property are neighborhoods being seized and leveled for the benefit of a shopping mall developer who build it on the grounds that it will generate higher tax revenue for the government. Social property is the seizure of the fruits of personal and private effort by government for its own benefit in the name of an imaginary people, but that's actually for the benefit of the government hierarchy and their friends who will use and abuse and despoil this now public property as it suits them with limit or concern about either social or ecological justice.

Sam Morrison: So. We can safely conclude that neither private nor social property has a clear place unless somehow mediated in a Green Republic. And we have to find a new category of ownership and property.

Wang Li: Clearly, the lesson is about the importance of maintaining the dynamic balance between freedom and community. Freedom without the balance of community leads to excess and exploitation. Community without freedom leads to oppression.

Sam Morrison: What's really on offer here is to find ways within the context of private property, social property, common property, and personal property to strike a balance where the outcomes reflect the equilibrating forces of freedom and community expressed ultimately as social and ecological justice.

Phil Clark: Personal property is different from private property?

Sam Morrison: I suggest it's a valid distinction. I know a Buddhist monk named Tree whose possessions seemed to be a bowl for eating and offering, a pair of sandals, a robe or two, and a toothbrush. My cat has her bowl. My turtles their tank. Intimate modest personal property is different from the one thousand pairs of shoes of a rich fashionista. We each have a right to minimal necessities that are not items for commerce.

Phil Clark: That's a fine point of clarification. But on a large scale, addressing private, social, and common property, it is participatory and democratic forms that establish the structures that protect and nurture both freedom and community so both can exert their necessary voices and functions.

Wang Li: So neither private or social or common property can be allowed to run roughshod in the name of bundles of rights claimed for a particular property regime.

Sam Morrison: What's optimal for all types of property is self-management based on forms that balance rights and responsibilities.

Phil Clark: Again, we cannot underestimate the potential importance of the three sections of Article One on ecological conduct to establish the principles and parameters for the ownership and management of property. As Elinor Ostrom pointed out, common property regimes worked well without imposition of government if exercised by those directly and intimately involved with the right to use the common and the responsibility to maintain it.

Sam Morrison: Obviously, the air, water, and soil represents the global commons. The tragedy of the commons advanced by Garret Hardin supposes that without private ownership, the commons will be abused. That, unfortunately, has been what happens to the atmosphere and water that's allowed to be used as a sink for pollution under industrial business as usual, both in market and nonmarket manifestations.

Pentti Aalto: Yes, it's stunning how much global carbon and other toxic air and water emissions are both regulated and considered legal. The nature of much administrated pollution regimes is to grant pollution for free up to certain amounts. And while one smoke stack or exhaust pipe spewing exhaust as permitted from fossil fuel combustion may be tolerable, hundreds of millions of them are leading us toward global ecological catastrophe and self-destruction granted as a matter of right. I have a right to drive my car and fire my boiler if it meets requirements on rates of pollution.

Phil Clark: Property is the basis of the pollution fallacy. That the bundle of property rights, the right to use and enjoy property naturally as a matter of law, and indeed as a matter of natural right and freedom, naturally confers a right to legally pollute.

Sam Morrison: The Green Republic and Article One sharply circumscribe such a right within the requirement of action and financial gain meeting, also meaning the regeneration of natural capital.

Meagan Simons: And it's also important to note that such mandates are general. In a Green Republic, there is no entitlement to pollute. There is no right to pollute. No permitted aggregate limits or grandfathered entitlements to poison after which regulations or fees are imposed. There's no purchasing of rights to endlessly pollute in markets for carbon or for any other pollutants. This is relevant on all scales and all levels and in all ecosystems.

Pentti Aalto: By saying no purchasing of rights to endlessly pollute, you seem to leave the door open a little for hard and quickly diminishing cap and trade programs as a transitional market step for some polluting substances and processes.

Meagan Simons: Yes, I did. But that's a quick way of getting from here to there. This worked with chlorofluorocarbons that could be firmly controlled with production of the most dangerous agents halted and strictly monitored. That's not the same as attempting to control hundreds of millions of fossil fuel burning point sources as a matter of right.

Pentti Aalto: Indeed. And there are also things like assessments placed on land that increase with the degree of development on the land that instead of the practice of taxing land on the basis of highest potential use, place assessments on land on the basis of actual use which means that so-called raw land is rewarded and untaxed as natural land.

Phil Clark: That's a use of a modified Georgist scheme for ecological ends. In terms of what's permitted and what's not following Article One, processes that have zero pollution, zero depletion, and zero ecological damage by capturing outputs and using it for inputs for other processes are what's encouraged. In this sense, you can use coal for energy on the pollution question if there were zero emissions, if the gases and waste were used for other things.

Bob Irving: Wait a minute. Georgists scheme like my uncle George?

Sam Morrison: Like Henry George who proposed a single tax based on rental value for undeveloped land that would capture the value added by efforts throughout the economy that raised such rents. The value of renting an acre in midtown Manhattan is a whole lot higher than on the back roads of Salisbury, New Hampshire. Not there would be too many acres of vacant land in Manhattan outside of public parks. You would have to determine what would be the rent on an acre of land in a given place, given no real comps for raw land. Whatever the rental value, you had nothing to do with that increased value of your acre of land that was the product of hundreds of years of hard work. Here, the suggestion diverges from George's plan by tinkering with it based on ecological ends.

Phil Clark: Obviously, zero depletion from fossil fuels is, in practice, almost impossible, as is zero depletion from much else, even silicon, that's not renewable.

Sam Morrison: That's why renewable processes are what's maximally encouraged, and processes that lead, on balance, to ecological improvement and the regeneration of natural capital with nominal negative consequences.

Wang Li: When you speak of net and nominal, you've open up a crack big enough to drive a coal or nuclear power plant through.

Pentti Aalto: That's certainly true. That's why the Green Republic cannot just rely on Article One to be honored largely in its violation and breach. It can be like the cynical deceit of the Nazis with the words *arbeit nacht frei*—which means, "work brings freedom"—on the gates of the Auschwitz extermination camp. They also delivered the poison gas in the back of a truck painted with a red cross. What's relevant is the social construction of ecological market rules sending clear market signals for sustainability, the systems of rules, laws, and regulations that subject all processes to ecological tests, incentives, and disincentives within a system of strong democracy, participation, empowerment, and self-management.

Meagan Simons: This agrees with what I am suggesting in the larger sense. The Green Republic is about balance and feedback. Much as we are talking about balancing freedom and community through democratic means, we are balancing property rights and natural rights with property duties and natural responsibilities. For every right, there must be a countervailing responsibility as well as a feedback means to equilibrate and balance those rights and responsibilities to help create and maintain a healthy balance, or system state.

Sam Morrison: That's the test for property regimes in the Green Republic. Any bundle of rights is balanced by a bundle of responsibilities and a means to effectively equilibrate both. The intent is to understand the system state, and to facilitate effective action and encourage self-management as the expression of freedom and community. The results—the proof is in the pudding—contributing to the practices of social and ecological justice and making economic growth mean ecological improvement, the regeneration of natural capital as well as the growth of finance capital. This is real wealth, the triple bottom line of sustainability manifest in the ecological, the economic, and the social.

Phil Clark: That's the dream. It's important to recognize that the Anthropocene, the Age of Pollution, has been characterized by a reduction, as Eric Freyfogle points out, to land as property and people only to a supposed broad market cash value. The ecological value of the land in the local ecosystem is held as valueless, as is the work and efforts of people unless they are paid cash for it.

Meagan Simons: Somehow, we have created the worst of all worlds. A market cash dependent economy that holds ecosystems valueless, and the use of the land as basic locus for food, water, shelter, and fuel is viewed as an anachronism. Local knowledge and skills, self-reliance, and self-management and community is valueless outside of cash transactions. The Green Republic is, in part, about rescuing the application of markets and the potential efficiencies, freedom, and self-management opportunities they present from the reductionist trap of devaluing both natural capital and community.

Sam Morrison: The Green Republic appropriately revalues natural capital and community in an ecological market system.

Ruth Johnson: Land is not just an abstract idea. Land is life. Land is the steep, steep Tennessee hillside acres that a farmer let my Cherokee ancestor farm when she walked off the Tail of Tears, the forced march of Native Americans removed from their land and homes and forced to march to Oklahoma. Land is the Tennessee farm my grandfather Pap farmed. He farmed the old way. By hard work, with manures and natural fertilizers. With mules and horses and not machines. Raised his big family and entertained and cherished his many grandchildren. And still was able to save enough money to provide for his disabled daughter for the rest of her life. I remember shouting matches between Pap and my uncle W. A. about adopting "modern" farming methods. Pap, who almost never raised his voice and never raised his hand, refused to listen to W. A. and adapt "modern" farming methods of chemical fertilizers and buying machinery like most people were doing. Pap was not going to put money in the pockets of the bankers and the chemical companies. He trusted, cherished, and fed his land and his family, and banked and invested as much money as he could. He was a man who grew up hard, beaten with a chainsaw by an alcoholic father, and instead, he unclenched his fists and followed an oath of love, peace, and duty on his land and for his family and community. My grandmother told me she only saw Pap drunk once when he came home drunk and yelling from a party. She locked the door, and he had to sleep in the barn. He never drank again.

Wang Li: Economy in the traditional Greek sense was *oikonomia*, household management. An ecological future means, in part, a return to the practice of prudent management on all levels including, and particularly, that of the local. For the general is fundamentally shaped and influenced by the sum of local inputs and influences. That's why the struggle for an ecological future must be waged and won one ecosystem at a time.

Phil Clark: Yes. It's both a scientific and economic absurdity not to value ecosystems. Destroy the ecosystem. We have destroyed the economy. Destroy one local ecosystem, and we have destroyed the ongoing and renewing economic, social, and ecological benefits from that ecosystem. What price can we put on the value of evolutionary potential and coevolution? What if our common ancestor, for all placental mammals, no longer egg layers, Juramaia sinensis, was destroyed in China along with its ecosystem 150 million years ago? The supposed rights to property must be conducted within the limits of ecological duties and responsibilities.

Wang Li: We are establishing the broad constitutional principles that enable and facilitate the expression of the local struggles for prosperity and sustainability ecosystem by ecosystem, community by community, where the understanding of a community and of its health is ecological, economic, and social. A three-legged stool.

Meagan Simons: In a Green Republic, we restore the explicit and implicit value of land. The ability for all not just to receive income flows, but to use the land. Thus, food can be produced at home or by neighborhoods, whether in traditional gardening or farming, or in urban vertical agriculture. Water can come from a dug or drilled well on your land, or by capture of rain through cisterns, and capturing and using runoff from rainstorms instead of sewering.

Sam Morrison: That's the aspiration, and the Green Republic is the means. Obviously, like the difficulties of the Arab Spring made clear, it's very difficult to go from long-term tyranny to working democracy; it's also difficult to go from industrial business and pollution as usual to a functioning ecological civilization in one jump. And therefore, the good and the better cannot be forbidden because it's not perfect.

Wang Li: Yes, this is about changing trajectories, imperatives, rules, and feedback loops on all scales. Article One: The Ecological Imperative, is the beginning, not the end. A declaration can be inspiring and bold, but a declaration's ultimate importance must be determined by action, not just words.

Bob Irving: A Green Republic can't just be about an organizational and process chart.

Pentti Aalto: Think of the Green Republic like a large passenger jet whose pilots go through detailed checklists as a routine matter before they fly. And sometimes even though they do that faithfully, they make a mistake, and don't pay attention to all their instruments and outside conditions. If they had, the plane would have left the ground and reached cruising altitude safely. But sometimes they miss something, and there's a crash, sometimes a devastating crash that the investigators call pilot error. It wasn't that they deliberately wanted to crash, or that there was a major equipment failure, or a freak wind phenomenon. It was, instead, a failure to pay close enough attention, a failure of feedback systems to take corrective action quickly enough.

Bob Irving: The Green Republic cannot be created as human proof.

Pentti Aalto: Yes. There's no technological marvel to be relied upon with a MTBF—Median Time Between Failures—that's infinite and self-healing, that runs on autopilot forever.

25. Technological Questions

Phil Clark: That's why it's extraordinarily difficult to build so-called inherently safe nuclear plants. Because the technology isn't inherently safe. It's nuclear plant operators or airline pilots that sometimes step in and avert catastrophe. The pilot who safely lands a passenger jet in the East River in New York, or the nuke plant superintendent who disobeys orders from Tokyo and averts nuclear meltdowns in another nuclear complex south of the doomed Fukushima reactors.

Meagan Simons: The long-term success of the Green Republic rests on the unquantifiable human factor in pursuit of sustainability. This, ultimately, will come from the unscripted practice of improvisation, of bricolage, cobbling together solutions from what's on hand, both materially and socially, from both individual and collective effort.

Pentti Aalto: We can build what seems to be inherently safer nuclear plants with the understanding that if something goes wrong, there will be hell to pay. Like at Fukushima where the tsunami breached the seawall, and the earthquake damaged cooling pipes. The calculated risks said this was a minuscule and acceptable risk. Obviously, this is a classic example of failure and technological arrogance. It's easy to make risk assumptions when probability estimates provide desired results—whether that means safe or not or too dangerous.

Meagan Simons: Technological arrogance I think has two aspects. First, there's the unwillingness to appropriately consider the consequences if something goes wrong. In Boston, there was a great molasses flood when a huge tank holding molasses collapsed unleashing a flood of molasses fifteen feet high and 160 feet wide moving at thirty-five miles per hour that killed twenty-one people in the North End. The pictures of devastation look startlingly similar to me to the ruined Fukushima reactor buildings after the tsunami and hydrogen explosions. The difference was water washed the molasses away. Second, there's also the unanticipated consequences of our technological brilliance. We didn't anticipate the destruction of the upper atmospheric ozone from supposedly inert CFCs.

Pentti Aalto: The consequences of fossil fuel pollution have aspects of both not appropriately judging the known risks and not fully anticipating the consequences. For fossil fuels, a limited number of point sources of pollution if properly limited seemed innocuous. With a billion exhaust pipes, we are risking global ecological crisis and the destruction of our civilization.

Bob Irving: Way too much of a good thing. If we can sell a thousand cars with internal combustion engines, why not a million? And if a million, why not a billion?

Pentti Aalto: Unfortunately, like much of what we do in the Age of Pollution, the consequences are not examined beforehand. Instead of a precautionary principle before the use of new processes and new chemicals, the typical path for many things is try it and then prove that something's wrong before anything is done about it. Yes, a new prescription drug, a new pesticide, a new nuclear plant, a new car design has to be vetted as a consequence of all too clear experiences of disasters and an existing regulatory regime. But there's a remarkable amount of acquiescence in allowing new chemicals and new manufacturing processes to enter the ecosphere with little or no examination of consequences beyond cost and profit.

Phil Clark: There are two keys in helping understand and judge future performance. First, what's the highest goal, and second, how can this be enforced. If the highest goal is safety and ecologically sound conduct, and every participant has the right and the duty to correct problems, then the possibility of safe and successful operation dramatically increases. If the main purpose is operation throughput for profit, and we are considering a nuclear complex built on the seacoast in an earthquake and tsunami zone, then welcome to the Fukushima nuclear catastrophe. The same is true about questions of scale and ecological impact.

Pentti Aalto: Yes. It turns out that safety and outcomes are very much driven by goals. The US Navy, for instance, has an enviable safety record for training landings and takeoffs from aircraft carriers. Safety is the primary concern in an inherently complex and dangerous activity. Every crewmember from the pilot on the bridge guiding the landing to the flagmen on deck has the ability to cancel a landing or takeoff if they see anything amiss. Safety is the controlling concern. Each participant is empowered to take definitive action even in the hierarchical military setting. But the safety record is quite different in combat missions where the mission, not safety, is considered paramount.

Phil Clark: That's why in a Green Republic the preeminence of clear ecological goals, manifest in social and ecological justice and supported by empowered individuals and communities in a strong democracy, is central to the life of an aspiring ecological civilization attempting to build the road as we travel.

Bob Irving: Democracy is not just a nuance to have added, an option if you can afford it.

Phil Clark: But we're recognizing that an undemocratic hierarchical order—like the military or a one-party state given clear goals—mandates, and the empowerment of individuals to act to help achieve ecological ends, like the Navy trying to land planes on aircraft carriers, can be similarly effective.

Sam Morrison: I agree. There is no single path toward a sustainable and ecological future. I think that the Green Republic can balance freedom and community in ways that achieve ecological ends successfully and escape the stultifying order of a unitary hierarchical system. But, in principle, there's no reason that hierarchies cannot accomplish ecological ends.

Wang Li: The danger, of course, is that strong hierarchies, like the Navy, are unusually dependent upon their leader's willingness and the ability to continue to pursue ecological goals, and their continuing willingness to permit what would be an otherwise unthinkable level of discretion for those involved in particular activities to raise ecological questions.

Meagan Simons: The succession problem of unitary hierarchies is a tendency toward sclerotic corruption, of "bad emperors" to succeed enlightened and beneficent despots.

Phil Clark: Nero, after all, was quite popular with the Roman masses challenging the power of the senate and their pretensions while providing bread and circuses. A Donald Trump for his time. The problem with hierarchical orders without democratic choice is that it inclines to family dynasties and not to meritocracies.

26. Green Republic: Athens Not Sparta

Sam Morrison: But the Green Republic's concern is, so to speak, the revivification and improvement of Athens, not of Sparta.

Meagan Simons: It's also true that a prince of Machiavellian mien might be quite effective at the pursuit of an ecological path from narrow power maximizing self-interest.

Phil Clark: Yes, we are fortunate in that the pursuit of ecological survival is not limited to democracies of high moral character. It can also be imposed and guided from above by the regimes of emperors and their secret police. The same is true of a wide range of systems that do not follow the multiparty democracy model.

Sam Morrison: We are not attempting to develop a general theory of building an ecological civilization. We are trying to develop a usable model for a Green Republic. Our concern is not the nature of other possible models beyond the recognition of some of the common dynamics and problems that other paths present. Again. Our focus is the health of Athens, not the viability of Sparta.

Wang Li: We recognize, then, the potential ecological success of the single-party hierarchy under circumstances of clear goals, broad empowerment for pursuit of ecological ends throughout the system, and the mechanisms for meritocracy to somehow guide succession and maintain ecological goals.

Phil Clark: The same success and problems, of course, can afflict party democracies with each election cycle. The victory of the Coal Party would be more than a minor blip.

Meagan Simons: That's why we are talking about a constitutional order based on Article One: The Ecological Imperative and the broad distribution of power throughout the social order to help balance the forces of freedom and community and achieve social and ecological justice.

Phil Clark: The constitutional structure is meant to permit conflicting programs and varying points of emphasis in pursuit of ecological ends and social justice. There can be a right wing program, a centrist program, left wing program, a Green program, a Deep Green program, and so forth. In Britain, the Conservative Party came to power and advanced their own take on achieving global warming goals. This is far different from a new government rooted in climate denial and industrial business and pollution as usual.

Sam Morrison: The succession question is perhaps more daunting without transparent democratic means that are able to successfully have a transmission of ecological goals. How can you be able to reach across leadership successions with sufficient institutional memory on continuity? And this raises the question, can we have a one-party democracy that has these kinds of mechanisms?

Ruth Johnson: In Louisiana, they have nonpartisan primary elections. These could be applicable to all sorts of systems without parties as well. All candidates run in the first election. If no candidate receives more than 50 percent of the vote, the top two candidates have a runoff election. There's nothing, in principle, here to say that elections of this sort couldn't guide succession in single-party hierarchical states, or if not determining succession, help assume ecological continuity.

Wang Li: Nothing except the unwillingness of those in power to give it up in terms of control of the succession, or a willingness to be term limited. But a constitutional order could require such things as term limits, succession choice, and ecological continuity though democratic means while not recognizing political parties and organizing outside of the system.

Sam Morrison: Clearly, the tendency is for mature hierarchies to have the choice of leadership made by the ruling circle, the politburo, or the imperial senate picking the first among equals. This typically evolves from brute struggle for power and violence into the more orderly and less bloody choice by the elites. This is usually a far different process than democratic means. But there's nothing that prevents conditional use of democratic means, such as elections in Iran where the elected government leadership is still subject to the will of the Supreme Leader the Ayatollah.

Wang Li: China has made the decision to build an ecological civilization, to make economic growth contingent on ecological norms, to be a world leader in renewable technologies, in electric vehicles and batteries, HVDC power lines to move power, in high-speed rail, in sustainable international investment. China has also lifted hundreds of millions from poverty. All this under the leadership of the Communist Party.

Sam Morrison: China is clearly pursuing another path than that of the Green Republic we are considering here. China, if it embraces nonparty electoral mechanisms, does so on the basis of the Communist Party and meritocracy. What's crucial here is to adopt rules and policies, electoral or not, to help ensure the ongoing support of ecological ends.

27. Supporting Ecological Ends

Phil Clark: China faces the same problem that was confronted by the American founders like Madison in the constitutional post-revolutionary era—a considered distaste for factions and the triumph of special interests over the common good, and the development of political parties. We now take political parties as the *sine qua non* of democracy, and of party platforms, that may or may not be a guide for potentially comprehensive changes in policies.

Sam Morrison: The irresistible imperative of parties is to gain power though organizing coalitions and appealing to voters in whatever electoral forum exists, formal or informal, elite or universal. Systems that afford proportional representation, of course, encourage the proliferation of parties and of coalitions, and the sharpening and focusing of a party's message. Winner-take-all electoral systems, by their nature, discourage the growth of multiple parties and, in practice, trend toward two-party systems.

Pentti Aalto: *Federalist No. 10* addressed "The Utility of the Union as a Safeguard Against Domestic Faction and Insurrection." In the founder's republic, democracy would be confined to the limited purview of a constitutional republic structured through appropriate power limiting checks and balances between executive, congress, and jurists. The prize for winning control of the federal government would be limited. Direct democracy and the mass expression of popular sentiments and passions would be strictly limited.

Phil Clark: Both James Madison and Xi Jinping have similar feelings about factions and political parties. Where they differ is in Madison's judgement that "liberty is to faction as air is to fire," and therefore sought the only way to limit faction without extinguishing liberty, which he was unwilling to do. Instead, Madison embraced the structure of a large and diverse constitutional republic with strictly constrained and limited democratic powers. This is not the path chosen, so far, by China.

Sam Morrison: We await with interest the result of the Chinese ecological experiment.

Meagan Simons: From the standpoint of the Green Republic, is there a particular form of democratic process that's inherently desirable? Assuming its constitutional order is guided by an Ecological Conduct Article One, does it make a difference if the system encouraged multiple parties in a propositional parliamentary system, or two parties in a winner-take-all system with a strong president? Additionally, there are a number of ways that both proportional representation and democratic empowerment could be encouraged under what otherwise would be a strong chief executive two-party system. Or are all matters essentially second order questions, assuming as a given a strong central government with limited distribution and participation in power? Why not a confederation model with more strictly limited central power and greater local empowerment?

Sam Morrison: For the Green Republic, we are presupposing An Ecological Conduct Article whose goals are of central importance. Then we are posing four questions. First, how do we build an ecological future through the conduct of democratic means for the pursuit of sustainability? Second, how to make the growth of financial capital also mean the health and regeneration of natural capital? Third, how to pursue the achievement and maintenance of social and ecological justice? Fourth, how to make the understanding of the practice of a fiduciary responsibility work for sustainability and for social and ecological justice?

Wang Li: This is central. Details are just that.

Phil Clark: The details are where the devils lurk.

Pentti Aalto: The judgement here must be focused on the ability of any arrangements to foster strong and persistent democratic processes that express the maintenance of a durable balance between freedom and community, between natural rights and natural responsibilities, for the needs for expansion and growth with limitation and repair.

Wang Li: In Han China, Dong Zhongshu, in a famous memorandum to Emperor Wu, helped lead the radical reform of the government guided by Confucianism and the practice of a harmonious universe with the emperor as a central balancing point between the heavenly, human, and early realms. This was the tool seized by Wu for radical reform of court and bureaucracy that helped establish a four-hundred-year period of stability in China under the Han dynasty. Similarly, our Article One and the principles of the Green Republic are our own Dong Zhongshu memorandum. Dong Zhongshu wrote to the emperor:

> Confucius said, "Rotted wood cannot be carved, a wall of manure cannot be whitewashed." Now the Han has succeeded the Qin, but China is like rotten wood or a wall of manure: though you wish to govern well there is no way it can be done. You pour forth laws and outrages spring up; you send down ordinances and deceit arises. This is like cooling a boiling pot with hot water or using sticks to beat out a fire, things only become worse … Poetry says, "Serve the people, serve the gentlemen; blessings shall come down from Heaven." If you govern so as to serve the people, blessings will surely come from Heaven. What a true king should cultivate are the five norms of *ren*, righteousness, ritual, wisdom, and faith. When these five are embellished blessings will come down from Heaven and the magic of the spirits will assist you …

Sam Morrison: Yes, in our own fashion, a Green Republic is the means for consolidation and long-term stability and prosperity to define our own spheres of righteousness through the pursuit of sustainability and the practice of social and ecological justice.

Wang Li: The choice is between radical instability and collapse, or a stable, prosperous, and renewing social order. The Green Republic is a radical, but essentially reformist strategy, that for existing multiparty market democracies, transforms economic growth from a self-destructive to constructive force, embraces and strengthens the realms of both freedom and community, and maintains social and ecological justice central.

Phil Clark: What's not to like from left, right, center, and green provided...

Bob Irving: ... provided what?

Sam Morrison: Provided it can be done. And our job is to consider pathways to that successful end.

Bob Irving: And those details about electoral mechanisms are of interest, but not by themselves at the heart of things.

Meagan Simons: No, I think not. They are significant and of interest, but are relevant mostly in historical context. I don't think we're telling two-party systems, go proportional. Or proportional systems, go two-party. But we are saying there are structural reforms and changes that can be employed to facilitate good governance.

Sam Morrison: Yes. It would be simple enough to move from winner-take-all voting for both the legislative offices and the chief executive. Voting can be proportioned by lists in classic style, or second choice voting could be allowed to more fully reflect democratic opinion. In second choice voting in a contest with multiple candidates, voters would pick a first and second choice. Instead of awarding the victory to the candidate with the plurality of votes, or require a run-off election for the top two candidates, if no one achieves 50 percent on the first vote, votes would be transferred to each voter's second choice. This would continue until one candidate achieves 50 percent. It certainly makes sense in an indirect election for a president based on winner-take-all state electoral votes to award electoral votes by plurality of congressional districts, thus reducing the real prospect of a minority president winning the electoral vote, but losing the popular vote.

Phil Clark: All these concerns are true enough. But at bottom do they really matter for the success of a Green Republic?

Sam Morrison: I would say they do. And they matter in a fashion that includes, but also transcends, the constitutional arrangements for the Green Republic. While of central concern again, it is not the fine details of specific systems. These are worthy of attention to assure a viable and fair democratic political process. But the crucial question is the existence and maintenance of multiple and diverse sources of power throughout society that prevent abuses of power leading to the failure of the ecological project.

Phil Clark: Immediately, by rejecting a one-party state, you are automatically broadening the locus of power. But that, by itself, does not automatically lead to democracy. Egypt, after Mubarak, when given the opportunity to vote, chose Morsi, an Islamist who was swiftly deposed by military with encouragement by the revolutionaries who had led to toppling Mubarak. This led, unfortunately, to the reestablishment of strong man. Political democracy must be accompanied by strong forms of political and economic democracy throughout the social order. This is meant to provide a broad and diverse expression of political economic self-interest throughout a Green Republic that would make the swift imposition of a military dictatorship, or abandonment of the ecological path, unthinkable. Economically, there is the power of organized workers and their unions, of self-managed cooperatives, businesses, and cooperative banks and credit unions, broad ownership of assets from housing, to schools, to other social institutions. The more people who have meaningful skin in the game, the more likely the health and dynamic nature of the democratic process and the stronger the political and economic power from below in support of social and ecological justice. That's what will make the Green Republic a durable success dependent not upon one leader or one election cycle, but rooted in the fabric of many complex, dynamic, and free communities.

Bob Irving: Politics in the Green Republic cannot be a matter of conversations at the billionaires' ball.

28. Tools for Social and Ecological Justice

Sam Morrison: Let's examine our social and ecological justice tool kit.

Phil Clark: Let's.

Pentti Aalto: With due regard for creative and market base mechanisms, I hope.

Meagan Simons: Emily Dickinson wrote that hope is a thing with feathers. And I hope our hope has substance. And feathers.

Ruth Johnson: Indeed. Otherwise it's not worth the time.

Sam Morrison: First, I think we need to recognize that great inequality is at the root of social and ecological injustice. Our world, where sixty-two billionaires have as much as half the world's population, and a sixty-million-to-one disparity and wealth is an absolute predictor of gross injustice.

Phil Clark: After some multiple of resources between rich and poor—whether it is five to one, six to one, twenty to one, one hundred to one—any social system is likely to be characterized by broad disparities of both wealth and power expressed by social and ecological injustice for the poor majority that both benefits the rich and encourages the ever-worsening disparity of resources and their abuse.

Bob Irving: Abuse stokes and feeds power at the expense of justice, ecological and social.

Ruth Johnson: The disparity between rich and poor matters fundamentally when the one, whether five to one or a hundred to one, no longer have access to a good life, to good food, clothing, shelter, clean water, health care, education, a healthy environment, recreation, retirement, and cultural resources that are a basic human right for all.

Meagan Simons: This is the world of the aristocracy and impoverishment, of Russia under the czar, of the slave cotton kingdom of plantations. A tiny owner class, a modest number of useful foremen and slave drivers, builders, and merchants, and then the mass of the people organized into multiple degrees of impoverishment and hopelessness.

Phil Clark: It's neither fair, just, or ecologically sustainable to say, I made my billions honestly in a free market and have my right to enjoy my property and wealth.

Pentti Aalto: So your ecological solution is just to tax me and take my hard-earned property and capital to subsidize those who didn't work hard enough or smart enough to do what I did.

Phil Clark: Not hardly. But in pursuit of sustainability and ecological and social justice, the only path for long-term survival and prosperity is for all of us to have the opportunity to live sustainably.

Meagan Simons: This means sustainability and long-term prosperity requires the use of long-term measures to decrease inequality and help establish social and ecological justice as a common reality for all.

Sam Morrison: This does not mean the need for the abolition of markets, of forced equality and uniformity. It means the recognition of several basic facts of life. That market failure exists. This is more than the need to free market mechanisms from influences so they can function freely where an invisible hand will make all well. Market failure writ large is also the consequence of financial speculation in mortgage backed securities and credit default swaps betting on them that brought down the global economy.

Phil Clark: Banks and speculators largely to be bailed out by the taxpayers.

Pentti Aalto: And no perp walks for accounting control fraud.

Phil Clark: Not a one.

Sam Morrison: So market failure also means social failure, the inability of markets to maintain and reestablish by themselves acceptable balance. The choice presented by the Goldman Sachses of the world to the politicians was, of course, the absurd statement of "too big to fail."

Pentti Aalto: What that should have meant in my market heart instead of "too big to allow to collapse," was "stabilize and liquidate." The market is really good at pricing distressed assets. The taxpayers could have guaranteed all deposits and recapitalized the banks, if necessary, to make real business loans. This would have meant bankruptcy under Chapter 11 for reorganization. The stockholders would have been wiped out as would the unsecured bond holders. The senior executives would all have lost their jobs, and many referred for criminal action for accounting control fraud. The recapitalized bank would have been broken up into sensible chunks and sold. Real business lending, not incomprehensible financial speculative instruments, would be their business. What we have instead is a market system designed to privatize profits only and socialize the losses following speculative collapse.

Phil Clark: And the high-risk carousel continues spinning.

Sam Morrison: Yes. A system guaranteed to produce small, steady, and expanding profits by insiders with their computer algorithms and ever-evolving creative gaming of markets, punctuated by black swan events, as described by Nassim Nicholas Taleb, a number of standard deviations from the allegedly normal course of events. The inherent problems with dynamic markets dealing with imagined financial products is that it is an open system subject to all sorts of unanticipated circumstances—one dependent upon assumptions made by complex financial models—leavened by fraud.

Pentti Aalto: Like getting financial rating agencies to classify bundles that they called tranches, of sub-prime dreck, as AAA investment grade.

Meagan Simons: While Aristotle sagely noted that an unexamined life is not worth living, the behavior of financial markets is that unregulated or poorly regulated financial markets are a sure road to disaster.

Sam Morrison: The practical lesson for the Green Republic is that if there are to be markets, they must be operated within a market structure in accord with the ecological imperative, including its pursuit of ecological and social justice, and be carefully and prudently regulated. This means a structure that combines a desire for maximization and prudent limitation.

Pentti Aalto: And democracy strong enough to watch the regulators, and preventing both abuse and regulatory capture.

Sam Morrison: Indeed.

Phil Clark: We need two kinds of basic mechanisms to help level the playing field and keep it that way both within and between nations. This means, from a global perspective, lessening inequality both within the richer nations, and transferring wealth and technology from rich to poor to assist in all being able to follow a sustainable and ecological path.

Meagan Simons: A classic exercise in ecological development as an expression of enlightened self-interest. Markets as tools for both raising the poor from poverty and into prosperous and sustainable economies that benefit all economically, ecologically, and socially.

Sam Morrison: This was the logic behind the Marshall Plan that supported the rebuilding of European economies following the Second World War that was an enormous success in all aspects.

Ruth Johnson: But now, aid is criticized as giveaways to dictatorial kleptocracies, or following military geopolitical concerns.

Pentti Aalto: This is not just a liberal versus conservative question, or a market versus socialist issue. Market-based conservatives recognize that market failure exists and that there needs to be mechanisms other than revolution or the abolition of markets for all of us to be afforded the opportunity to live a decent life. Hence the idea of a basic income grant or a negative income tax is a concept that has been advanced by decidedly right wing politicians like Richard Nixon and economists like Milton Friedman, typically as a replacement for other social welfare programs and their bureaucracies. Existing earned income tax programs are a more constrained version targeted at working families.

Sam Morrison: It's crucial to understand the Green Republic and social and ecological justice as not just an expression of the left versus the right.

Pentti Aalto: The long-term question for the existence of markets of any type is ecological sustainability for which social and ecological justice is an indispensable concomitant in the long run for the continued existence and flourishing of the Green Republic.

Bob Irving: Or else it will spiral out of balance and need to rely upon authoritarian means to save itself.

Wang Li: Therefore, the pursuit of social and ecological justice is not a high-minded costly add-on. The Green Republic in Article One: The Ecological Imperative mandates that we give up our polluting ways and that a market system must operate to turn away from lower cost pollution, depletion, and ecological damage by both monetizing the consequence of self-destructive behavior, and erecting a structure of market rules, regulations, laws, and good practices that mediate against these choices outside of law and democratic constitutional framework.

Bob Irving: It's unconstitutional! That's a fundamental full stop objection.

Pentti Aalto: And part of this grand bargain to eschew self-destructive industrial conduct by all, by both rich and poor, is the provision of the pursuit of social and ecological justice for all.

Sam Morrison: Brazil has implemented the Bolsa Familia to supplement the income of poor families. This has apparently accomplished its intended goal not just of income support, but community and family solidarity and continuity by relieving some of the root struggles for subsistence and instead allowing families to pursue means and strategies to improve their lives.

Pentti Aalto: Not just live off the dole.

Sam Morrison: There are several factors at play that the Green Republic must consider. First, is income support basic and general for all without regard for income, assets, or work? Or is it supplementary, like a negative income tax or earned income credit and means tested? Second, does the right to a basic income require some community service responsibility, or good works? Is it a reward for some period of national service, military or nonmilitary, for all who are able? Or is it a basic entitlement of a citizen? Third, should such a grant be considered as a one-time birthright? Like Thomas Paine suggested in response to accidents of birth and property awarded to all at age twenty-one or eighteen to be used as desired or for targeted purposes, like education. And, fourth, of course, is how will this be paid for?

Pentti Aalto: Two things. First, a portion of the money, the trillions produced by Sustainability Credits (SCs), could be directed toward a universal basic income grant. This can simply be monetizing a fraction of SCs on the books of a basic income bank that would allow investment in renewable projects or efficiency projects producing more SCs that would generate cash to be able to fund the basic income grant. This is the manna from heaven approach. Second, if this does not happen, I think we best approach this from the standpoint of the Green Republic as a universal employment system—where work is available for all, that jobs are shared, good education and training is universal, workers are transferred to other enterprises instead of being laid off. The context is that a basic wage is a living wage that education and training is a lifelong opportunity.

Sam Morrison: The maximization of production and consumption is not the primary aim of a Green Republic. Inherent limits of ecological conduct and the pursuit of social and ecological justice place a series of material and consequential limits on economic activity.

Meagan Simons: But the pursuit of sustainability also places philosophical limits on conduct that supports the dynamic of freedom and community within the context of social and ecological justice to allow people to make choices for their lives and families other than more consumption.

Phil Clark: That such an option is a philosophical choice does not mean it is one that must or will be made.

Pentti Aalto: Such are the consequence of freedom and community in motion that permits a variety of choices within a system rooted in justice and fairness and sustainable prosperity.

Phil Clark: This cannot happen within our existing system of radical inequality and a sixty-million-to-one ratio of wealth between the richest and poorest. But in a Green Republic with a ratio between richest and poorest of five to one, or ten to one, the embrace of freedom and community facilitates the varied exercise of freedom to shape lives and communities.

Sam Morrison: The context of a Green Republic is abundant and affordable renewable energy resources that power a system aspiring to zero pollution and zero waste where economic growth means ecological improvement. The technology in such a system will tend toward customized production through information technology producing goods to order through 3-D "printing" using sustainable materials.

Pentti Aalto: It's unclear to what extent work in the twentieth century sense of full-time employment for wages will continue to be relevant in a twenty-first century world where much production is reduced to programming, scanning, and printer maintenance? Where factory work is robot work. The relevance of a basic income grant or negative income tax is clear in such a world of great material wealth where each citizen has a right to a share of the gross product in exchange for meeting designed responsibilities.

Bob Irving: The right to a share need not be the right to an equal share. The right is to a basic share, and you are incentivized to do more to have more if you want more. More and more that I see as a home builder is no longer craft work, but programmed machine work and some human assembly work. Stick-built houses are becoming an anachronism.

Pentti Aalto: In this robotic 3-D printing world, the tendency under inequality as usual is for the deepening of the gap between an ever-larger mass of the poor and deskilled service and manual workers, burger flippers, and nail clippers with a tiny elite of owner entrepreneurs and an ultra-consuming class of programmer technocrat, AP designers, machine repair technicians.

Phil Clark: Of course, the burger flippers, nail clippers, coffee baristas, and bartenders can be replaced by future generations of robots.

Meagan Simons: The power of this technology can be the gateway to an enormous increase in craft, art, philosophy, scholarship, games, sport, and creative action of all sorts in the context of a basic income grant or negative income tax where a living wage makes pursuits other than wages possible for all and establishes large domains that are ecologically harmless. This is a world beyond work as we understand it, not a world of mindless boredom, but a productive and vital world.

Sam Morrison: The Green Republic is a way to manage and shape the transformation to a world where humanity's concern transcends earning money in the face of the enormous sustainable productive capacity of our eco-technology combined with the pursuit of social and ecological justice.

Pentti Aalto: Today, the most popular jobs for graduates from elite schools are app design and social media development. Twenty years ago, it was investment banking. This reflects both the central nature of information as the high profit center of the twenty-first century and beyond and the dematerialization of production and consumption in the face of global ecological challenges and the essential pursuit of sustainability.

Wang Li: Information—not physical commodities, not oil—is the crucial resource of the Green Republic and the basis for sustainability as practice of an ecological civilization.

Ruth Johnson: It is the recognition of this new underlying imperative that will lead to the opening of eyes and embracing the implications for work, life, and love posed by the ecological imperative as central for the Green Republic and for our futures.

Phil Clark: The folk singer Charlie King, whom I met in the Clamshell Alliance, had a wonderful song that comes to mind: "My life is more than my work, and my work is more than my job."

Charlie wrote, "So look around can't you see, we are not rich or sane or free, it all depends on you and me, not on some leader's dream..."

Sam Morrison: Those days stay with you, don't they?

Phil Clark: The lessons of standing up and speaking truth to power do.

Meagan Simons: That's what the Green Republic is about, a collective willingness to speak truth and embrace new paths for the expression of freedom and community through democratic means.

Bob Irving: I like the basic income grant. When can I expect the first check?

Sam Morrison: It's sort of like social security. It's a long time coming. But when it finally arrives, suddenly there's a real floor you're standing on.

Phil Clark: That's also what this is about. We've managed, along with incredible creation of material wealth, to create an enormous amount of poverty. Poverty not just because some are richer, but because we have foreclosed the opportunity for lives organized around unequal cash exchanges in the market, and, what's worse, cash exchanges frequently organized around activities that are polluting, depleting, and ecologically destructive.

Sam Morrison: The Green Republic is the reassertion of choice, of the triumph of freedom and community over industrial business and pollution as usual. Ecological destruction is shown the door, and ecological sustainability within the context of social and ecological justice is shown in.

Bob Irving: The world organized for the pleasure of billionaires is not only unfair, but is the world we have built though radical inequality and is radically unsustainable.

Phil Clark: It's the world of resource wars for oil and natural gas. Soon to be the world of wars for water and for food unless we act swiftly to decisively and permanently stop and reverse the march toward climate change and ecological catastrophe.

Sam Morrison: The Green Republic is one of those decision points of inflection where we can choose a different direction that will represent an increasingly different future than a continuation of business as usual. It cannot be reduced to the triumph of social democracy. It's an expression of the rise of both social and ecological justice. Looking out for a generation or a hundred generations or a hundred thousand generations is the time frame we must engage in the pursuit of sustainability.

29. Sustainability and the Social

Meagan Simons: What's particularly interesting and challenging about the Green Republic it that is the deliberate social manifestation of sustainability as a conscious social process. The saving grace of the Anthropocene is the practice of sustainability to make human action lead to the health and regeneration of natural capital manifested by thriving ecosystems.

Phil Clark: Humanity's leap from its fortunes as just another species among the myriad to our ability to exert influence of geophysical import must take the next step to focus and channel human action and its consequences toward sustainable ends.

Wang Li: The pursuit of sustainability by the Green Republic is a conscious manifestation of the new social nature of the fundamental ecological dynamic of sustainability where life that exerts healing a coevolutionary force upon planet and ecosphere to help create and maintain conditions maximally suitable for life.

Sam Morrison: The Green Republic is a biosocial entity, a manifestation of Gaea, as Lovelock suggests, as a living organism with enormous coevolutionary power, the application of human means and technique toward ecological ends.

Pentti Aalto: Requisite humility is called for in that we have tampered with Gaea to the point of beginning to unleash a sixth mass extinction, disrupting climate cycles heretofore the province of the influence of volcanism and perturbations in the earth's orbit.

Meagan Simons: We have no choice then to take ourselves seriously as biosocial entities, as an integral part of both the web of life and able to make conscious contribution to the pursuit of sustainability shaping human action on all levels to sustainable ends.

Pentti Aalto: This means not just intent, but the requisite feedback loops to allow human action to be adjusted and calibrated to achieve ecological ends.

Phil Clark: What this means is a different understanding of human needs and necessities and desire.

Ruth Johnson: This immediately leads us to leap to the economic and the factory system. Whether Blake's "dark satanic mills," or something that appears much more benign, where renewably powered robots do most of the work.

Bob Irving: You mean it's time to raise questions—what's the purpose and meaning of all this technology beyond the self-justification of more to fix the problems we've created without technology.

Phil Clark: Evermore.

Meagan Simons: What purpose indeed. Why not ever-less?

Sam Morrison: Like a writer pursuing concision. The greatest impact with the fewest words.

Meagan Simons: A Hemingway and not a Faulkner.

Sam Morrison: I was thinking more poetry and less technical manual. Of human scale. Of the beloved country. Of peace and freedom.

Meagan Simons: If ecological survival and prosperity is predicated upon limits and expanding the bounds of freedom and community released from ecological threat, why not make limitation job one? Think before we act. The default position becomes less instead of more.

Pentti Aalto: This is the emergence of Article One: The Ecological Imperative as social reality.

Phil Clark: We view production and consumption with more a jaundiced eye.

Bob Irving: Wait a minute. You're calling shopping into question.

Phil Clark: Put it this way, view production and consumption with an artist's eye.

Ruth Johnson: Find the beauty in the present moment and the wind riffling through the leaves and our feet caressing the ground as we walk.

Phil Clark: But we've hitched the ecological wagon to the ecological global growth agenda. Haven't we? Millions and millions of solar panels and wind machines.

Wang Li: Yes, of necessity we need to build the tools for the new sustainability infrastructure.

Sam Morrison: Yes. We have to replace the tools of pollution with the tools for sustainability.

Phil Clark: And then don't we have to continually replace them in a twenty – or thirty – or forty-year cycle?

Sam Morrison: The opportunities for economic dynamism are enormous and ongoing. But an ecological future is also about stepping back from maximization and embracing limits for social as well as ecological reasons. Ecology drives necessity. The social and economic drive choice.

Pentti Aalto: And you're suggesting that there is no essential conflict between profit seeking and more production and consumption of ecological goods or their social manifestation.

Sam Morrison: Yes. But that's true within the context of Article One: The Ecological Imperative that includes the pursuit of social and ecological justice as crucial.

Ruth Johnson: But an ecological civilization must be about more than better factories, sustainable factories, more production, and beneficent machines.

Meagan Simons: Is our goal of the Green Republic for everyone to have their own 3-D printer, able to produce almost any aspect of our desires using software and sustainable inputs and powered by renewable energy?

Phil Clark: That's a future almost like the wasteful society in Paul and Percival Goodman's *Communitas*. Endless production of goods roll off the assembly line and drop into a ravine.

Sam Morrison: If we can have anything, this cannot mean we should have everything. That's the *Sorcerer's Apprentice* world of production unleashed. Even given sustainable inputs and renewable energy.

Pentti Aalto: Are we talking about limiting the number of 3-D printers produced? Like we limit carbon dioxide released? Or talking about limiting time you have access to the machine or what and how much can be produced by the machine?

Meagan Simons: An ecological civilization is also about the cultivation of restraint, the embrace of limits, of art, play, and love as opposed to the maximization of production and consumption, getting and spending. Yes. Practical limits are placed on what is discouraged from the 3-D printer world.

Pentti Aalto: By limits, you don't mean a society of rationing, of green police, and neighborhood watchers reporting secret consumers? What if someone or many someones don't embrace these limits?

Meagan Simons: By limits, I am embracing a social and cultural behavior that's a product of behavior, informed by education and social style, and backstopped ultimately by Article One and the ensemble of organizational and social forms, market rules, and policies that support it. The Green Republic is a democracy. Neither an ecological civilization, nor limits spring to life fully formed the goddess Athena herself from the head of Zeus. Nor did it roll off the assembly line.

Phil Clark: An ecological civilization, like an ecosystem is shaped by, is a reflection of its history, circumstances, and many mediating and interacting processes.

Bob Irving: One of which is democratic politics. That opens a large realm of choice and uncertainty by its nature.

Phil Clark: We can't write, or predict, the history of an ecological civilization before it happens based on current existing conditions.

Sam Morrison: Yes, the Green Republic is contingent upon circumstance and choice. It social, human, political, economic, philosophical. It's informed by choice and value. Of these choices and values are limits. Limits are expressed in all arenas. For instance, a circular economy here is also a matter of insulating human and ecological values from the endless maximization of production and consumption.

Meagan Simons: That's all about saying enough is enough.

Bob Irving: By teaching ourselves and our children well. Not by guilt, or by lust and greed, but by the embrace of transcendent values of art, sport, religion, contemplation, exercise, community, cooperation.

Meagan Simons: An ecological civilization makes these choices for limitation because it can. And those are social choices. Not dictates from the palace.

Bob Irving: Look at it this way. Before huge gas-guzzling SUVs like the Lincoln Exterminators covered the roads, for many years, there were things like the Suburban. A giant vehicle that was only occasionally bought by large suburban families and sport team coaches. And then suddenly it became fashionable to drive bigger and bigger vehicles. Maybe it was 9/11 or wars for oil or what, but cars got bigger and bigger. And then suddenly it flipped as gas prices rose and sanity returned, at least for a while. Regulation can require limits on gas consumption that will affect what's built. But consumer choice is choice. And it is only democratic action and education that can inform and limit those choices.

Meagan Simons: We hope to be heavy on the education. But Article One will also drive the shape of what's to come and condition the nature of choices and our individual and efforts.

Pentti Aalto: A free market. But one with ecological market rules.

Meagan Simons: To the extent our democracy allows.

Phil Clark: Limitation means first to slow the speed of the mad avariciousness and redirect our energies toward sustainable ends.

Sam Morrison: Yes. Enough. Less and no more. But it's not just about counting and throughput.

Ruth Johnson: This is very much an example of the pursuit of excellence or quality, what the Greeks called *arete*, virtue or excellence. Giving the best of ourselves to move toward honor and away from shame.

Meagan Simons: In our ecological civilization, where our intentions are focused on more important matters than consumption and production, buying and selling.

Phil Clark: Who will wield the whip?

Meagan Simons: No one, obviously.

Sam Morrison: That's freedom and community in action. The free community of free communities, an ecological civilization.

Meagan Simons: That's the task of the ecological civilization.

Phil Clark: The gleaming city on the hill.

Bob Irving: More the modest home in the dale.

Meagan Simons: In a pleasant and healthy land without limit on a planet of healthy habitat, leading from one habitat to another without end as you travel around our planet, one healthy community and ecosystem leading to another. Unity in Diversity. Freedom and Community.

Phil Clark: So. Who aspires to be the billionaire President of General Ecology?

Sam Morrison: Not I.

Meagan Simons: Not I either. And I expect that's not what drives any of us.

Phil Clark: What about those who do want that job?

Sam Morrison: That's why the Green Republic is about building an ecological civilization, an expression of life, liberty, and the pursuit of happiness in the twenty-first century and beyond rooted in social and ecological justice. We don't need billionaire executives while 50 percent of children and those under twenty-five in many neighborhoods live in poverty.

Phil Clark: The Green Republic aspires to be the manifestation of a society of free and equal citizens. Free in fact, not just in theory.

30. Industrial Business to Ecological Business as Usual

Meagan Simons: You could say that the basis of industrial business as usual was a system that maximized production consumption, profit, and externalities. Profit then was directly related to the creation of externalities, meaning:

$$\text{Profit} = \text{Ecological Pillage}$$
$$\text{And in this system,}$$
$$\text{Maximizing Profit} = \text{Maximizing Externalities}$$

Pentti Aalto: But limits were imposed since the consequences of maximizing externalities became all too clear.

Bob Irving: And environmentalism arrived.

Meagan Simons: In a Green Republic:

$$\text{Maximizing Profits} = \text{Minimizing Externalities}$$

In a Green Republic, the connection between the growth of production and consumption is entirely conditional upon consequences. Thus, there is little practical limit in selling information in myriad forms in a renewably powered cyberspace as a potential high volume, high profit center.

Phil Clark: One simple equation:

$$\text{Maximizing Profits} = \text{Minimizing Externalities}$$

Becomes a corollary to,
Maximizing Profits = Minimizing Expenses

As externalities rise, so does a system of assessment on those externalities—as well as the imposition of simple limits. This is central to the continued success of a Green Republic. There must be a clear and strong market price for pollution, depletion, and ecological damage.

Pentti Aalto: The ability of market systems to function ecologically must rest upon the practice of the simple relationship. Maximizing profits = minimizing externalities.

Sam Morrison: This is the basic identity relationship that is elaborated upon and optimized by the dozens of business schools and finance. It is this equation:

Maximizing Profits = Minimizing Externalities

It is the golden road for profit and the lifeline for the survival of dynamic market systems.

Phil Clark: It's a self-deluded pretense to believe that market systems can continue to function on the basis of the creation of negative externalities that socialize, shift, and externalize true costs to society, the ecosphere, to those downwind and downstream and to future generations.

Meagan Simons: The practice of maximizing profits = maximizing externalities is the poisoned road to self-destruction and ecological collapse and market collapse.

Sam Morrison: The Green Republic guided by the pursuit of sustainability and the equation that maximizing profits = minimizing externalities is the hardnosed business solution to the ecological crisis. No more and no less.

Phil Clark: But that begins to address the question of why have markets? Why condition human effort by the competitive chase for money, by commodification of all aspects of human life, the reduction of all values to cash market values? Aren't there ways to make effort be guided by goals that are not simply mediated by cash and market success? That does not mean operating without budgets or financial constraints, but the market alone in command dissolves social value.

Meagan Simons: This is what Marx memorably said when looking at the power of markets over social life and social structures. He wrote, "All that's solid melts into air."

Pentti Aalto: An ecological market system is a social creation that need not embrace the commodification of all aspects of human life and the reduction of all values to market values. Such is the risk of markets. Much as totalitarianism, or fascism, is a risk of command economic systems and can be potentiated by the concentration of political and economic power in nonmarket systems.

Sam Morrison: The ecological imperative and its commitment to social and ecological justice creates a structure that, by its nature, addresses on an ongoing basis the dynamic balance of freedom and community. It is freedom and community in action that will place limits on the scope and consequences of market action in social, political, and economic forms. The ecological market of the Green Republic uses the creativity, freedom, and incentives of market forces but in the context of sustainable action.

Meagan Simons: The ecological market of the Green Republic could incline itself, for example, to the growth of a strong cooperative sector, to the practice of an associative democracy where there is democratic ownership and participation in a broad range of activities, not just in business, but housing, schools, farms, institutions of all sorts.

Phil Clark: The backbone of the Green Republic must lie in an empowered, active, and informed citizenry facing the power and challenges posed by markets and by the pursuit of sustainability.

Pentti Aalto: Markets must be embraced as a tool with requisite constraints for social and ecological justice. A means to an ecological end. Not an end in itself. Sustainability is an amorphous term. Like sustainable profits. But when you understand that sustainability entails social and ecological justice, it becomes much clearer that this is not just based on business as usual or meeting the new boss, same as the old boss, as the Who famously sang.

Phil Clark: But to an extent we are still wrapping cotton candy around markets. Again. Why can't we just have a plan within the context of self-management and decentralized democracy based on your Article One: The Ecological Imperative?

Wang Li: I think there's no principled reason that you could not make such choices. But, in practice, I think that in a world where market forces prevail along with the complex social forces of ownership, investment, and employment that surrounds markets, it's an enormous challenge to start by saying we will abolish markets, ownership patterns, and employment and substitute our managed nonmarket system.

Sam Morrison: There are inherent problems in nonmarket systems of the creation of nonproductive bureaucratic fiefdoms, of the creation of the "new class" as Milovan Đilas, Yugoslav vice president under Tito, said of nomenklatura managers, of double-dealing, nepotism, bribery, and corruption. The new class of mangers replace the old class of capitalists as wielders of power.

Meagan Simons: I remember an interview I read between Václav Havel and a Politburo member. Havel was still an activist, not yet president of the Czech Republic. The official told Havel that even though he was the number two man in the marketless hierarchy, he felt little personal power in shaping or fundamentally changing the nature of events. The system and its character overwhelmed individuals and community. Freedom had evaporated, and community served the maintenance of an inflexible tyranny that was inefficient, unjust, and far from optimal in almost all aspects.

Bob Irving: Market systems are no more immune from corruption and abuse than nonmarket systems.

Sam Morrison: The ecological world of the Green Republic with its practice of full shared employment, basic income grant, or negative income tax manifested in and combined with the pursuit of social and ecological justice will tend to transform and change the dynamics of markets and provide effective levels of insulation from the intrusion of market forces in all aspects of life.

Phil Clark: But what's crucial is that such countervailing forces and democratic means persist and withstand the forces that markets unleash. The prospect is for existential security to be our common experience. Market systems are based on the prod of work or starve, or at least work or live in poverty and misery, and people often work and live in poverty and misery.

Meagan Simons: If a living wage as part-time employment in the context of social and ecological justice could support creative expression as a common thread of life in the Green Republic.

Pentti Aalto: Is this just another social democratic fantasy that will prove too expensive to fund and fall victim to competition from cheaper labor not burdened with the weight of paying for such expensive indulgences?

Meagan Simons: No. We have a real opportunity to create a durable ecological order that enormously expands the ambit for freedom and community and opens the door for varied and expansive choices that transcend the imperatives flowing from market rules and market order.

Phil Clark: I'm a professor at a state university governed by public budgets and student tuition and paid according to merit and degree of skill and knowledge. Nevertheless, the university is still market driven to please the students, and not unnecessarily antagonize the paying customers. I grade according to a student's performance.

Sam Morrison: I also spend some of my time teaching, which I sometimes enjoy thoroughly, and sometimes not, and doing research which is my passion. Yes. There's pressure not to fail students who tender the faintest efforts and to inflate grades on a normal curve. But in a nonprofit institutional setting, we are still essentially governed by market or market-like imperatives.

Wang Li: The paycheck is still your reward.

Sam Morrison: Yes. And university politics here are sometimes viscous since, as they say, the stakes are so small. So I must admit a convergence between the world of the market and the world of the university. It's not an enlightening prospect for the future Green Republic.

Bob Irving: Well, the disabilities of the market and nonprofit institutions are not the limit of our imagination.

Ruth Johnson: I hope not. The human spirit deserves better.

Meagan Simons: What rough beast, its hour come round at last, is slouching toward Bethlehem to be born?

Sam Morrison: Indeed. Correlation is not causation. The future is not yet decided. That's why we're here considering options.

Phil Clark: There's a lacuna between aspiration and reality.

Wang Li: We can only start from a sense of where we are, trying to understand the prospects and possibilities of a Green Republic in pursuit of sustainability.

Meagan Simons: That clearly means different things to different people.

Sam Morrison: I think it's more useful for the Green Republic not to view organized human action as either governed by market or nonmarket forces. The specific social structures and norms governing market or nonmarket conduct are more significant for lived human experience. On one extreme, we have a hypermarket like that in the play *Glengarry Glen Ross* where workers earn money only from commissions and their abilities to convince customers by any means necessary. The boss is the sales manager who tells the workers, "It's as simple as ABC, always be closing," and introduces a contest for the workers. First prize, a new Cadillac; second prize, a set of steak knives; third prize, the door. We could also assume that the homes they are selling are toxic and built to collapse quickly as soon as the fresh coat of outgassing paint wears off.

Bob Irving: Sounds like a large developer who hired me to build the cheapest houses with the cheapest materials, but to look good enough since you couldn't see the walls of particleboard.

Sam Morrison: We can also work at the State Enterprise Number 17. This is a place where they pretend to pay us and we pretend to work. We do get paid. Poorly. The boss's concern is not sales, since there's little real demand for our shoddy manufactured housing. It's either falling apart as near instant slums, or the pieces remain unassembled in storage since no one wants to use their income to buy them. There are stores, typically empty of anything people really want to buy like good food, good clothes, or quality goods. Of course, the materials are toxic, dangerous for the workers and the people who buy the finished product.

Bob Irving: The point is that both market and nonmarket systems can be soul dead and toxic.

Wang Li: And we could debate which is worse, but that's not what we are trying to accomplish.

Sam Morrison: Exactly. I think that within the context of an ecological civilization, the experience in both market and nonmarket forms can both be acceptable and substantially similar. Suppose we have a well-established organization manufacturing a socially useful product, let's say a baby monitor. It has many orders from longstanding customers for its product. In a Green Republic, the experience of most of the workers here is fairly similar in market and planned environment. Yes, there are market stresses placed on sales and management that may get transmitted to the workforce as a whole. But these stresses are mitigated substantially by the full employment, part-time if necessary, combined with basic income or negative income tax.

Wang Li: Yes. Here the influence of market forces is mitigated and the market failure of an organization is not a catastrophe, just an example of the life cycle of organizations and changes in technology, habit, and use.

Pentti Aalto: In these circumstances, Schumpeter's notion of creative destruction by market forces means the destruction of organizations, not of the people and communities they represent.

Phil Clark: The Green Republic's success is predicated on a comprehensive structure of limits and feedback loops to control and limit the impact of market forces.

Wang Li: The model for workplaces combines aspects of forces like codetermination in Germany where workers and their unions have seats on corporate boards, and that of entrepreneurial cooperative social systems like the Mondragon Cooperative system in the Basque region of Spain, where cooperative businesses are supported by a co-op bank, a cooperative entrepreneurial division, co-op science and research, co-op educational institutions.

Pentti Aalto: In Germany, the tradeoff for codetermination is an open shop where workers are not required to join a union. And the system you're describing calls for limitations on relocation of jobs and factories to search for cheaper wages and lack of ecological restraint.

Sam Morrison: That's true. But the context of codetermination and cooperative ownership forms and the flexibility of jobs throughout the economy means that organizations and communities are not just fungible expressions of capital assets. Businesses are not able to be simply transferred across the globe leaving the factory, the workers, the community behind in the search for lower wages and lax ecological restraint. The model is:

$$\text{High Profits} \neq \text{High Externalities} \neq \text{High Capital Mobility} \neq \text{High Labor Mobility}$$

Meagan Simons: What you're suggesting is that the Green Republic is also an expression of the ecosystem, in part, as social. That the living world must be addressed in a fashion that encompasses its social manifestations.

Sam Morrison: This does not mean that organizations necessarily deserve the same consideration, respect, and regard as a species. But it does mean that the disruption of social systems can have profound consequences for ecosystems and their health.

Phil Clark: The principle of unfettered markets with little or no regard to ecological or social consequences is that:

$$\text{High Profits} = \text{High Externalities} = \text{High Capital Mobility}$$

Externalities here mean both ecological and social which are encouraged by high capital mobility, the right to separate capital from community and workers, since workers and community have no ownership stake.

Wang Li: This is obviously remedied by cooperative enterprise. In particular, this can be remedied by large cooperative type systems of many small companies able to form dynamic alliances to develop new products and respond to changing conditions such as in the Emilia-Romagna region of Italy, near Milan-Bologna and Rimini-Ravenna. A couple of thousand cooperatives with sixty thousand workers and tens of thousands of small companies cooperate intelligently on a local level and can compete on a world scale. It's an unusual combination of strong local democracy and successful small business cooperation.

Phil Clark: The question to me is can the structure and nature of the Green Republic allow for the generalization and reproducibility of something vaguely comparable to the successful Mondragon and Emilia-Romagna models reflecting differing social and cultural circumstances?

Meagan Simons: The success of the Green Republic is predicated on the dynamic strength and sufficiency of political, economic, and social structures to maintain the balance between freedom and community to facilitate the operation of the Green Republic. We can't forecast accurately the texture of complex social arrangements. All we can do is make provisions to facilitate creative choices.

Phil Clark: So what happens when your Green Republic runs into the Kingdom of Pollution?

Sam Morrison: Obviously, there cannot be a lone sustainable island in a world of mega-pollution and ecological collapse. We're asserting that for a viable future for our civilization that the Anthropocene must mean the growth of an ecological civilization as successor to the pollution era. A Green Republic is one manifestation of an ecological civilization rooted in strong democracy and a market system pursuing sustainability and social and ecological justice.

Pentti Aalto: One of the roles of the Green Republic is to help the world pursue ecological ends. This means the embrace and application of the principle that growth of finance capital = minimizing externalities = regeneration of natural capital need be by law, by custom, and by practice embraced as common conduct.

Sam Morrison: To facilitate this transformation, there must be a transfer of knowledge, technology, and capital from the rich world to the poor. Global ecological transformation cannot occur unless the impoverished billions are enabled to pursue their dreams for a better life using a sustainable pathway.

Pentti Aalto: If we all tried to live like the US in the twentieth century, we would need the equivalent of three or four planet Earths.

Ruth Johnson: But we have only one.

Phil Clark: Hence the talk about missions to Mars. Or plans for geoengineering to make the planet habitable despite our polluting ways.

Meagan Simons: No. Hence the pursuit of sustainability and social and economic justice.

Bob Irving: Are you sure?

Sam Morrison: The transfer of knowledge and capital is not charity. It is investment, and it is a logical and necessary step in everybody's long-term best interest in ecological health.

Wang Li: Fundamental is a means to fairly raise and transfer such funds for ecological investment. To the point is the use of mechanisms like Sustainability Credits or an alternative such as the Basic Energy Entitlement, a BEE. The BEE begins with a sustainable per capita global entitlement of three tons of carbon dioxide a year per person. At that level, the amount of carbon dioxide released by seven billion people, twenty-one gigatons, would roughly balance the natural sinks for carbon dioxide, sequestered in soil and plants, used by photosynthesis, and dissolved in the oceans. Given the typical carbon intensity of energy use, this was roughly equivalent to seventy gigajoules of primary energy or 19,443 kilowatt hours equivalent per person per year.

Unfortunately, with atmospheric carbon dioxide now above 400 parts per million, as much as 50 percent of human atmospheric carbon emissions stays in the atmosphere.

Pentti Aalto: This means that even if we met the 19,443 kilowatt hours per year challenge, atmospheric carbon would still increase. We also need to remove two to three gigatons of carbon a year to reduce atmospheric carbon back toward preindustrial levels. This would mean sequestering carbon dioxide in biomass on land and sea and in soil. But in terms of the BEE, if you used more than seventy gigajoules of primary energy, you would be paying a BEE assessment.

Wang Li: Numbers. Numbers. I have some numbers on this.

Phil Clark: Data rears its head. Physics can be on the side of a sustainable ecological global growth and a sustainable investment plan catalyzed by a BEE.

Wang Li: The BEE assessment would be proportional to energy use with large industrial and commercial users paying much larger shares. The BIG (Basic Income Grant) would more than rebate BEE payments made by the poor in both rich and poor nations. US total BEE assessment for 311 million people at a penny a kWh equivalent rate would be around $300 billion a year. The average American, for example, would pay BEE assessments, while the average Chinese would be a net recipient of BEE transfers. An average US household using 7,200 kWh per year of electricity and driving a gasoline car 10,000 miles a year at 30 miles per gallon (11,303 kWh primary energy) would pay $72 BEE for electricity and $113 for gasoline a total of $185 per year.

Bob Irving: Wait a minute. Walk me back on this. Three tons of carbon dioxide per person per year. Seventy gigajoules of primary energy, or 19,443 kilowatt hour equivalents of primary energy. Tons of carbon I get. You burn it, you created it. And how does that equal seventy gigajoules of primary energy or 19,443 kilowatt hours? I also have no idea what a joule is. I know that I use six hundred kilowatt hours a month at my house. My car's a hybrid, it burns gasoline to create electricity. I'm measuring the kilowatt hours it produces?

Pentti Aalto: OK. In the effort to make a BEE simple, tons of carbon per person per year equals seventy gigajoules of primary energy, or 19,443 kilowatt hours per person per year. We've walked you into the high grass. Professor Hiller, you can make this clearer?

Phil Clark: I will try. If a BEE is not clear, how can anyone understand what it means and know what's useful and what's not, what's good and sustainable or what's polluting and negative, and how to measure and quantify our progress?

Meagan Simons: The analytic mind speaks.

Phil Clark: So. Let's start with tons of carbon per person per year. That's what's this is all about. A ton of carbon in this case does not have an energy equivalence beyond the conversion of all mass in the universe to energy applying Einstein's famous equation $E=MC^2$.

Bob Irving: That does not help.

Phil Clark: Understood. I couldn't help myself. Next time for sure.

Wang Li: We are counting on you.

Phil Clark: OK. Carbon dioxide is a nonflammable gas. It does not have a kilowatt hour equivalence by itself or represent an amount of energy measured in joules. The Basic Energy Entitlement (the BEE) measured in tons of carbon per person per year is the average amount of carbon dioxide released by burning fuels to produce the energy we need.

Bob Irving: In the houses I used to build before heat pumps and super insulation, you'd turn up the thermostat and the oil burner in the furnace would kick on and hot air would pour into the room while lots of hot gases, including carbon dioxide, went up the chimney.

Phil Clark: Burn a gallon of No. 2 fuel oil in your furnace and you will produce through combustion 22.4 pounds of carbon dioxide and release heat energy that's measured in joules, which is part of the dreaded metric system. Americans or Anglophiles who haven't gone metric use the Imperial British thermal units or BTUs, as a measure of heat energy. A BTU is roughly the amount of heat released from burning a wooden kitchen match from end to end. Burn a gallon of No. 2 fuel oil, and you produce 138,690 BTUs of heat.

Bob Irving: Quite a pile of matches.

Phil Clark: Now in the International System of Units (SI), the dreaded metric system, heat is measured in joules. A joule is equal to a small amount of heat, a tiny number of BTUs, 0.00094781712. A gigajoule is a billion joules, or 947,817.12 BTUs.

Bob Irving: Now it's becoming interesting.

Phil Clark: A gigajoule is equal to the heat of burning 6.83 gallons of No. 2 fuel oil. This means burn 478.1 gallons of fuel oil in your furnace, and you have used your total sustainable yearly energy entitlement.

Pentti Aalto: So, burn a gallon of No. 2 fuel oil in your furnace and you produce, in addition to 22.4 pounds of carbon dioxide that unfortunately goes into the atmosphere, about 138,690 BTUs of heat. Between 70 and 90 percent of that heat goes into your house, and the rest up the chimney with the carbon dioxide and other gases and smoke particles. Seventy percent heat into the house and 30 percent up the chimney if it's an inefficient burner system. Ninety percent of heat into house and ten percent up the chimney if it's a very efficient burner system. The 22.4 pounds of carbon dioxide is about 196 cubic feet of gas when it cools to 70 degrees.

Bob Irving: OK. I'm starting to get it. Light dawns on marble head. Burn a gallon of fuel oil, and that releases 22.4 pounds of carbon dioxide into the atmosphere and produces 138,690 BTUs of heat, some of which gets into my house and some of which goes up the chimney with the carbon dioxide.

Phil Clark: Yes.

Bob Irving: Now where do we get kilowatt hour equivalents? I sort of understand BTUs. But kilowatt hour equivalents?

Phil Clark: OK. A joule and a BTU are measures of energy. A joule, for physicists, is the amount of energy or work used to accelerate a body with a mass of one kilogram using one Newton of force over a distance of one meter.

Bob Irving: We don't need to go there.

Phil Clark: No, we don't. But what's really relevant for our purposes is that one joule is equal to one watt of power radiated for one second. There are 3,600 seconds in an hour. Yes?

Bob Irving: Yes. Sixty seconds in minute. Sixty minutes in an hour. I'm already starting to feel like Richard Feynman.

Phil Clark: One joule for one hour is equal to 3,600 watts. One thousand watts is equal to one kilowatt. Therefore, the energy of one joule for an hour, or 3,600 seconds, equals 3.6 kilowatt hours. A gigajoule is equal to one billion joules, and voila, one gigajoule is equal to 277.78 kilowatt hours. And seventy gigajoules per person per year means 19,444 kilowatt hours per person per year.

Bob Irving: But how do we get from kilowatt hours to tons of carbon dioxide?

Phil Clark: That's the key point. We are measuring the amount of energy generated by burning fossil fuels and releasing carbon dioxide. If there is no carbon burned, no carbon dioxide is released.

Bob Irving: So the Basic Energy Entitlement is assuming you are generating this energy by burning fossil fuels to produce the energy while producing carbon dioxide as a byproduct.

Pentti Aalto: Absolutely.

Phil Clark: So back to burning the gallon of No. 2 oil in your furnace. That produces 138,690 BTUs of heat. One BTU = 1055.05585 joules. There are 3.6 million joules in a kilowatt hour. One gallon of No. 2 equals 146.326 million joules, or 40.65 kilowatt hour equivalents. Since in the US we measure energy production by the heat rate or BTUs per kilowatt hour, let's get away from joules, and only talk about BTUs and kilowatt hour equivalents. One kilowatt hour is equal to 3,412 BTUs or, again, 40.65 kilowatt hours a gallon.

Bob Irving: So how does that get us to accounting for three tons of carbon per person per year?

Phil Clark: Burn that fuel oil to put heat into our house, we also put 22.40 pounds of carbon dioxide into the atmosphere. Burn 1,000 gallons a year, that's 22,400 pounds of carbon dioxide, or 22 tons right there. And three tons person per year is the limit to keep atmospheric carbon dioxide stable.

Bob Irving: Wait, if there's four people living here, we're down to 5.5 tons per person per year. But already way above three tons without talking about the lights, the car, hot water, my plane trips, everything I buy that's made in factories mostly powered by fossil fuels and delivered by trucks, trains, and ships mostly powered by fossil fuels. That's why the US is over seventeen tons of carbon per person per year. How can we ever get to three tons?

Pentti Aalto: That's where it gets interesting, and that's where the Green Republic also comes in. We're talking here about physical goals and how it can be done. But the Green Republic is all about making it so.

Bob Irving: I can tell you right out of the gate, I build low energy passive houses that don't use fossil fuels directly. They are affordable, super insulated with low infiltration and exhaust heat recovery. They're heated and cooled by efficient electric split systems, air-to-air heat pumps with a seasonal COP of 3.5—that's coefficient of performance, Sam.

Pentti Aalto: That means for every BTU in to run the heat pump that takes out of the air, three usable BTUs in energy come out.

Bob Irving: Heating and cooling year-round comes to 7,702 kWh. That's now about only 40 percent of our annual three tons per person per year carbon dioxide entitlement. That comes to 1.19 tons. If the electricity is coming from fossil fuel fired electric grid.

Pentti Aalto: And if the grid was powered by efficient renewables, the carbon contribution from primary energy here would be zero. Yes, that doesn't include the carbon contribution for making things and transporting them.

Meagan Simons: But if we use renewable power to charge our electric vehicles and run our factories, three tons per person per year doesn't seem pie in the sky at all. And the BEE we are talking about is designed to help provide investment capital to help finance the global transformation.

31. Electric Grid

Pentti Aalto: Let's consider the carbon components from the electric grid and how it contributed to our three tons per person per year carbon dioxide target. For the US, coal is the big one. But even without coal, there's still a big problem meeting our three ton per person target. We've already seen that the US coal power plant "fleet" of 1,309 coal plants produced 1.6 trillion kilowatt hours a year. Bituminous coal, or hard coal, produces about 2.07 pounds of carbon dioxide per kilowatt hour. That amounts to 1.6 gigatons of carbon dioxide per year, or 5.1 tons of carbon dioxide a person per year.

Phil Clark: By itself, US coal burned for electricity represents 8.9 percent of total global sustainable emissions of twenty-one gigatons of carbon. But the United States represents only 4.5 percent of the global eight billion plus population. Globally, coal amounts all by itself to 68.6 percent of total sustainable carbon dioxide emissions. Just burning coal takes up two-thirds of what is globally sustainable.

Pentti Aalto: Coal also represents 29 percent of total US per capita carbon dioxide emissions. We've also discussed how a ninety-billion-dollar investment a year for twenty years, $1.8 trillion over time, could replace all coal output with photovoltaics. Understanding we would use a blend of solar, wind, other renewables, storage, and HVDC power lines to effectively generate and deliver renewable energy to retire the coal feet.

Bob Irving: HVDC means?

Pentti Aalto: HVDC is High Voltage Direct Current. HVDC has much less power losses than typical AC lines which have more substantial power losses over long distances. HVDC makes it possible to move large amounts of renewable power from where it's generated to where it's used. By building networks of HVDC power, it's possible to create a very flexible and durable renewable power system over a continental scale.

Bob Irving: Why would we want to do that?

Phil Clark: It so happens that renewables over large distances tend to be inherently self-balancing. When it's windy in the East or North, it may be calm in the West or South. Photovoltaics, obviously, is a daytime thing. Wind tends to have higher output at night. On a continental or regional scale, it's possible to have a 100 percent renewable power system. The HVDC network that makes this possible to move power swiftly from where it's generated to where it's needed is key. That's one of the advantages of networked large-scale technology. Every house does need to be 100 percent self-sufficient all the time.

Pentti Aalto: This isn't just one huge super-grid to rule them all. The large-scale systems are part of a network that will include the millions and millions of small sources of distributed renewable generation that will become a part of almost every building and structure that will both draw power from the renewable grid and provide power to the grid.

Phil Clark: For example, your electric car can be plugged into your house circuit at night to charge. The car batteries can also, when needed and the batteries are sufficiently charged, provide power to your house and to the grid during times of high demand. Times of high demand will mean payment of high prices for stored or locally generated power encouraging sales and discouraging purchases. Times of low demand mean low prices for stored or locally generated power, discouraging sales to the grid and encouraging purchases from the grid.

Meagan Simons: You're describing a socially useful application of markets.

Pentti Aalto: Absolutely. What's key here is a fully loaded price for the electricity, all aspects, no externalities, like the cost of pollution, excluded from the price. It's a market composed of millions of large and small users able to respond to price instantly and optimize both the physical and economic efficiency of the system using short time price signals, say every five minutes, as the decision-making means.

Bob Irving: You mean I have to decide if I'm generating and selling or consuming and buying every five minutes and at what price?

Pentti Aalto: Not hardly. You've made the decisions beforehand when you chose the parameters on your control device. For example, your home PV system generating power from panels on your roof, and from your windows and wall PV, would always provide power to the house first. If there was surplus power, it would sell power back to the grid if the price was above $0.075 per kWh. If it was below 0.075, the surplus power would charge your battery system and then sell that power into the grid when the price was above $0.075 per kWh. The battery system was sized based on the amount of surplus power it would produce. $0.075 per kWh is the average price needed to get the power to make the battery system pay for itself in five years.

Phil Clark: Everyone their own mini-utility.

Sam Morrison: Yes, a far cry from the twentieth century utility of a handful of giant smoke stacks and nuclear plants. The efficient renewable utility is a tool to coordinate and optimize millions of generators and consumers networked together in a super-grid.

Wang Li: That is, in a fashion, an analogy to the operation of The Green Republic.

Pentti Aalto: And the system would also be much more secure from disruption. Whether from accident or malign intent.

Bob Irving: How so?

Pentti Aalto: Instead of a system being run by command signs being sent out from utility central.

Wang Li: Signals that could be hacked or blocked or sabotaged.

Pentti Aalto: The efficient renewable super-grid could be made substantially self-managing and self-balancing.

Phil Clark: Yes. It would be possible for each end use device or distributed generation unit, or at least each house or each meter, to have a controller that measures grid voltage and frequency. That doesn't lie. If the voltage drops 5 percent or is moving toward that, it would mean that self-generation would kick in or speed up, and device use would scale back or shed load or slow down. Set points on air conditioners might rise, water heaters would depend on storage. The same would happen if sixty-cycle frequency started to change. If the system couldn't correct itself, then the house would disconnect itself momentarily from the gird. If there was a local micro-grid for a neighborhood, the micro-grid would separate itself from the super-grid and then come back online using what local storage and self-generation resources it has, and your house would synchronize itself to the micro-grid with its own generation, storage, and reduced use program.

Bob Irving: We are starting to get deeper than I want to into the fine points of the super-grid and the dynamics of distributed generation and distributed control.

Ruth Johnson: But that's conceptually what the Green Republic is very much about, the balance between central and distributed operation and control with the choice made in general to privilege the local within the context of the functioning of the large system.

Pentti Aalto: And maintaining the balance of the system state.

Bob Irving: A smart balance is what we're looking for.

Meagan Simons: Chosen and maintained democratically.

Phil Clark: And not run by a high technological priesthood sending orders down from on high.

Meagan Simons: And not even if they were physicists?

Phil Clark: And not even if they were physicists.

32. Technical Complexity and Technological Evolution

Sam Morrison: The key for the unfolding of an ecological way is to inform technological choices by social imperative and social goals.

Meagan Simons: For us it's our Article One: The Ecological Imperative and its implications. The Green Republic arises from social choices that inform and determine how technology is developed and employed.

Phil Clark: For example, General Solar, Inc. could build and own a twenty-thousand-square-mile chunk of the West that could provide solar power for much of the Green Republic through a corporate-owned super-grid. And General Solar could also own all the distributed solar systems that are leased in a profitable fashion to people.

Meagan Simons: Our existing enormous disparity between rich and poor would, if anything, be worse. And while the technology might, in fact, represent an enormous decrease in pollution, depletion, and ecological damage, there would be a negligible improvement in social justice. It's likely that General Solar would not be as assiduous in the manufacture, installation, and recycling of their devices as we would desire. They have too much power both literally and figuratively.

Phil Clark: So it's not a technological imperative at work here of solar technology producing both a just and sustainable future. No, there could be legions of homeless seeking shelter beneath solar panels. Our sixty-two billionaires that now have more wealth than the 3.5 billion poorest could have more wealth than the eight billion in a world dominated by General Solar.

Meagan Simons: The prospects for a durable global ecological civilization in the world of General Solar seem vastly inferior and less likely than if a Green Republic was a common model and driving force behind the pursuit of sustainability and ecological and social justice.

Pentti Aalto: Strong democracy in the saddle is what must drive a successful ecological transformation. Doesn't need to be everywhere. But it should help keep everyone on the sustainable path. Much like strong unions raise wages all across the economy, including in nonunion shops.

33. Ecological Automation: Driverless Cars

Phil Clark: Driverless cars are another example of the kind of technological innovation and evolution we are discussing.

Pentti Aalto: Yes, the potential for driverless vehicles is interesting. It could mean many things.

Phil Clark: The rise of a society ruled and populated by technological automata.

Meagan Simons: The cars ultimately deciding things would be better off without the drivers.

Pentti Aalto: Assuming our machines can be maintained as our less-than-sentient allies, automated cars would mean more than being able to text while driving. There would be an enormous drop in crashes, injuries, and fatalities. There would also be much fewer traffic jams and less traffic congestion. It would also encourage car sharing. Cars could drop passengers off at multiple destinations, park itself, and then pick up the members of the car sharing group.

Meagan Simons: Cities could be made more walkable. Combined with improved internet services that facilitate online meeting, discussions, effective distanced communications, the need for commuting could substantially decrease, and the enrichment of communities to combine living, working, and playing would be much easier. Where you lived would become more a personal choice rather than driven by economic necessity.

Sam Morrison: The future nature of the self-driving vehicle remains to be seen and to be shaped by social choices, not just the question of maximizing sales and profits.

Phil Clark: The sustainability context is renewable electric power and how it's used. Whether it's for cars or high-speed rail or electric buses. There seems to be an irresistible desire to view transport as connected to your own car. Irresistible by car companies and their advertisements tied to your own car. Zipcar and Uber are examples of social sharing as opposed to private ownership. The self-driving car is the next generation of Zipcars. It makes little sense to view the future of sustainable transport as filling roads with a replacement number of private self-driving vehicles.

34. Global Forms

Sam Morrison: The Green Republic can be the form of a continental government, or a small city-state. An ecological civilization is predicated on the global spread of a variety of ecological forms shaped by social, historical, and ecological history and circumstance.

Phil Clark: To meet ecological ends, the scope of ecological actions must be global. This means new levels of cooperative forms on both local, national, continental, or transcontinental levels.

Meagan Simons: The Green Republic, it seems to me, can be more than the next step in the evolution of the nation state and its self-assertion. The Green Republic can be the basis for continental scale unions of multiple Green Republics collaborating as ecological entities. An American Union. An African Union. Ultimately, in an ecological civilization, a peace system will have replaced a war system.

Phil Clark: Yes. The global pursuit of social and ecological justice means a shared global prosperity. A convergence on sustainable norms. The devolution of armies to police, like Costa Rica. Strong local self-management and common ecological standards on a continental scale means under the subsidiarity principle, the aspects of the local and cultural are strengthened. Aspects of the nation-state are weakened and aspects of local communities and their capabilities are strengthened. Local communities, and their residents in this ecological world, have greater participation in ownership in all aspects of life including where they live, work, bank, heal, learn, play, and retire.

Sam Morrison: This is through a variety of forms, combing personal, cooperative, community, and corporate ownership with strong democratic and participatory features in all. This means a world driven by the fundamental principle of one person, one vote as opposed to one dollar, one vote.

Bob Irving: Sure. The corporations are going to agree to one person, one vote. Take my money please.

Sam Morrison: Democracy applied to corporations means first, codetermination where workers and their unions have seats on the controlling board where under Article One, fiduciary responsibility means the pursuit of the regeneration of natural capital as well as the maximization of finance capital and the pursuit of social and ecological justice. Second, new market rules that embrace no layoffs and reduced hours, and worker transfers combined with a BIG (basic income grant) or NIT negative income tax. Third, new financial instruments, under new market rules, that reflect variable yearly returns on profitable ecological investment and therefore do not entail the profit from the future labor of workers. Governance, in the one person, one vote noncooperative corporation, is by the vote of investors and by the workers apportioned for a share of the voting—for example, 33 percent.

Sam Morrison: The increased democratization of finance means increased local control of investment and the use of that investment for sustainable projects for sustainable communities.

Bob Irving: Democratic finance, other than credit unions and mutual savings banks, sound like another oxymoron.

Pentti Aalto: Not at all. Much capital is under social and at least nominally democratic control through pension fund investments that can certainly be subject to green investment under Article One and can be used to capitalize local and regional Green Trust Banks to invest prudently in sustainable projects.

Wang Li: As opposed to financial speculation and arcane financial instruments.

Phil Clark: How would such a strange creature of democratic finance work?

Sam Morrison: It would be capitalized by social insurance and pension fund money and by ordinary deposits and by ecological value monetized through Sustainability Credits. It would invest, following Article One, in ecological investments. Co-op and credit unions and new regional Green Banks would be governed by democratically elected local boards focused on local action. You don't need a trillion-dollar bank in New York to decide about investments in Keller, Texas. A North East Texas regional Green Bank covering counties from Nacodoches to Red River and Tarrant to Montague with a population of a few million that would elect the board and supervise prudent sustainable local investment.

Pentti Aalto: This is combined with the use of the Sustainability Credits (SC) or BEE, Basic Energy Entitlement, as a source for investment funds channeled through local democratic financial institutions. This establishes a virtuous global investment circle of funds raised by Sustainability Credits, and BEE assessment in richer, higher polluting nations becomes investment capital in local or regional democratically controlled Green Banks for local ecological investment as patient capital, and for investment in poorer nations. A portion of the revenue from this investment is returned to ecological wealth funds of the richer nations.

Meagan Simons: Globalization of the Green Republic also means the assertion of nations, by the Basques and Catalans, or the Kurds, for example, that are not limited to traditional states, but are more and more defined by common life ways and common experience and ongoing relationships. Subsidiarity means broad ability for local self-governance. The French and Spanish Basques for example, or the Turkish, Iraqi, and Syrian Kurds, are encouraged to practice self-governance. Nominally, the Spanish Basques are within Spain, the French Basques within France. But over time, as borders vanish and trade in information and cooperation increases, voluntary social organizations functioning across what are nominal borders supplant government actions with cooperative forms. For example, the Mondragon cooperatives in the Basque region of Spain have their own social security system that works in parallel with the Spanish and Basque self-government.

Bob Irving: The growth of the Green Republic as the model gets closer to the Jeffersonian idea of the government that governs best, governs least through the exercise of self-management, cooperation, and community ownership and investment.

Phil Clark: Self-identification will tend to be more with local community, and one's nation that can cross borders, than circumscribed within the nation state.

Meagan Simons: The nation becomes more like the cultural ecosystem and locus of action, identity and coevolution. The nation and the local community being the source of creative recombination, the practice of a cultural bricolage creating new forms and solving old and new problems in creative fashions. The nation does not need to be a discrete piece of territory and contiguous ecosystems. The ecological world is wrapped in the embrace of freedom and community in all its generative complexity.

Sam Morrison: The Green Republic, with the necessity of common global intent and cooperative action and aspiration, broadens the scope of freedom and community. The ecological context of a Green Republic is expanded global cooperation, a great increase in mutually beneficial fair trade in information globally, capital investment globally to help build the renewable resource infrastructure and the other tools for sustainability, and the development of global banking systems democratically controlled and making investments, not in financial instruments, but in the ecological transformation.

Phil Clark: The Green Republic can become the basic unit for the growth of continental scale unions based on cooperation and subsidiarity where strong local control is combined with broader decisions that move the whole toward ecological ends.

Wang Li: The broader context must be the global convergence on sustainability, and social and ecological justice, and the provision of resources at a mass scale in a global ecological growth strategy.

Meagan Simons: The Green Republic is the basis of the globalization of social and ecological justice as an expression of common self-interest as an emerging global ecological civilization.

Sam Morrison: I think that essentially sums it up what the Green Republic is and can become.

Phil Clark: What remains to be seen is action.

Wang Li: Yes action, not just theory.

Ruth Johnson: A plan that feeds the global spirit for ecological rebirth.

Pentti Aalto: For peace and prosperity.

Meagan Simons: For sustainability and ecology.

Bob Irving: For all of us, and for all living things.

Sam Morrison: What happens to a nascent Green Republic depends on each of us and all of us to build an ecological future together.

Selected Bibliography

1. First Problems

Hegel, Georg W. F., 1806. Phenomenology of Spirit: Preface Page 18. http://ndpr.nd.edu/news/24815-hegel-spreface – to-the-phenomenology-of-spirit

Yovel, G. W. F. Hegel, Yirmiyahu, and Paul Franco. 2005. "Review of Hegel's Preface to the Phenomenology of Spirit."*Notre Dame Philosophical Reviews*, July. https://ndpr.nd.edu/news/hegel-s-preface-to-the-phenomenology-of-spirit/.

Alexander, Christopher, Sara Ishikawa, and Murray Silverstein. 2010.*A Pattern Language: Towns, Buildings, Construction.* New York: Oxford University Press.

Fleming, Nic. 2014. "Plants Talk to Each Other Using an Internet of Fungus." BBC.com. 2014. http://www.bbc.com/earth/story/20141111-plants-have-a-hidden-internet.

Excerpt below:

Around 90% of land plants are in mutually-beneficial relationships with fungi. The 19th-century German biologist Albert Bernard Frank coined the word "mycorrhiza" to describe these partnerships, in which the fungus colonises the roots of the plant. In mycorrhizal associations, plants provide fungi with food in the form of carbohydrates. In exchange, the fungi help the plants suck up water, and provide nutrients like phosphorus and nitrogen, via their mycelia. Since the 1960s, it has been clear that mycorrhizae help individual plants to grow.

Fungal networks also boost their host plants' immune systems. That's because, when a fungus colonizes the roots of a plant, it triggers the production of defense-related chemicals. These make later immune system responses quicker and more efficient, a phenomenon called "priming". Simply plugging in to mycelial networks makes plants more resistant to disease... We now know that mycorrhizae also connect plants that may be widely separated. Fungus expert Paul Stamets called them "Earth's natural internet." ...

Simard now believes large trees help out small, younger ones using the fungal internet. Without this help, she thinks many seedlings wouldn't survive. In the 1997 study, seedlings in the shade – which are likely to be short of food – got more carbon from donor trees. "These plants are not really individuals in the sense that Darwin thought they were individuals competing for survival of the fittest," says Simard in the 2011 documentary "In fact they are interacting with each other, trying to help each other survive." ... other researchers have found evidence that plants can go one better, and communicate through the mycelia. In 2010, Ren Sen Zeng of South China Agricultural University in Guangzhou found that when plants are attached by harmful fungi, they release chemical signals into the mycelia that warn their neighbours.

Zeng's team grew pairs of tomato plants in pots. Some of the plants were allowed to form mycorrhizae. Once the fungal networks had formed, the leaves of one plant in each pair were sprayed with Alternaria solani, a fungus that causes early blight disease. Air-tight plastic bags were used to prevent any above-ground chemical signaling between the plants. After 65 hours, Zeng tried to infect the second plant in each pair. He found they were much less likely to get blight, and had significantly lower levels of damage when they did, if they had mycelia. "We suggest that tomato plants can 'eavesdrop' on defense responses and increase their disease resistance against potential pathogen," Zeng and his colleagues wrote. So not only do the mycorrhizae allow plants to share food, they help them defend themselves.

Casselman, Anne. 2007. "Strange but True: The Largest Organism on Earth Is a Fungus." Scientific American. October 4, 2007. https://www.scientificamerican.com/article/strange-but-true-largest-organism-is-fungus/.
This is a single organism that may be over 8,000 years old.

"The Worst Form of Government." 2017. The International Churchill Society. Churchill. March 20, 2017. https://winstonchurchill.org/resources/quotes/the-worst-form-of-government/.
Churchill on democracy: "Many forms of Government have been tried, and will be tried in this world of sin and woe. No one pretends that democracy is perfect or all-wise. Indeed it has been said that democracy is the worst form of Government except for all those other forms that have been tried from time to time..."

2. Freedom & Community?

Berlin, Isaiah. 1969. *Four Essays on Liberty*. Oxford: Oxford University Press.

- "Government that governs best, governs least" attributed to Thoreau and Jefferson, but first written by John L. O'Sullivan in *United states Magazine and Democratic Review* No.1 1837 On line: http://digital.library.cornell.edu/cgi/t/text/text-idx? c=usde;idno=usde0001-1" \n _blankUnited States Magazine and Democratic Review, no. 1 (1837): 6.

Boller, Paul F. 1995. *Not So!: Popular Myths about America from Columbus to Clinton*. New York: Oxford University Press. A discussion of this earlier source can be found in Paul F. Boller's *Popular Myths about America from Columbus to Clinton*.

3. Sustainability Rising

Piketty, Thomas. 2020.*Capital and Ideology.* Translated by Arthur Goldhammer. Cambridge, Massachusetts: Harvard University Press.

Bookchin, Murray. 1999. "Thoughts on Libertarian Municipalism." Institute for Social Ecology. August 26, 1999. https://social-ecology.org/wp/1999/08/thoughts-on-libertarian-municipalism/.

4. Manifesting First Principles of a Green Republic

Jensen, Derrick. n.d. "Derrick Jensen Resistance." Deep Green Resistance. http://deepgreenresistance.blogspot.com/p/derrick-jensen-resistance-radio-archives.html.Derrick Jensen's weekly Resistance Radio archives.

"Global Primary Energy Consumption." 2017. Our World in Data. 2017. https://ourworldindata.org/grapher/global-primary-energy.

Fell, Hans-Josef. 2012. *Global Cooling: Strategies for Climate Protection.* Leiden, Netherlands; New York: CRC Press/Balkema.

Schumacher, E. F. 2014.*Small Is Beautiful: Economics as If People Mattered.* New York, NY: Harper Perennial.

Daly, Herman E. 1991.*Steady-State Economics.* Washington, D.C.: Island Press.

Cobb, John B. 1992.*Sustainability: Economics, Ecology, and Justice.* Maryknoll, NY: Orbis.

Costanza, Robert. 1991.*Ecological Economics: The Science and Management of Sustainability.* New York: Columbia University Press.

Hawken, Paul, Amory Lovins, and Hunter L. Lovins. 1999.*Natural Capitalism: Creating the Next Industrial Revolution.*New York: Little, Brown and Company.

Amory Lovins has made many contributions on renewable energy, efficiency, and economics from his path breaking in Oct. 20, 1976 article in *Foreign Affairs* "Energy: The Road Not Taken?"

International Institute for Sustainable Development. n.d. "International Institute for Sustainable Development." Www. iisd.org. https://www.iisd.org.

International Institute for Sustainable Development website.

Meadows, Donella H., Dennis L. Meadows, and Jørgen Randers. 2004. *Limits to Growth: The 30-Year Update.* White River Junction, VT: Chelsea Green Publishing Company.

Limits to Growth in 1972 was a paradigmatic questioning of growth and business as usual. This was followed by a number of important, related works.

Boulding, Kenneth E. 1981*Evolutionary Economics.* Beverly Hills, CA: Sage Publications.

Kenneth Boulding was philosopher, peace activist, economist, prolific author of many relevant ecological economics books, and an iconoclast. The International Society of Ecological Economists presents an annual Boulding Award. (I should note that my article on Ecological Economic Growth posted by members of the ISEE was removed with prejudice from the ISEE website for daring to suggest that EEG was possible.)

Hicks, John. 1971.*The Social Framework: An Introduction to Economics.* Oxford: The Clarendon Press.

John Hicks's, a Nobel Prize-winning economist, extensive work helped define and quantify issues of income, consumption, and sustainability.

Georgescu-Roegen, Nicholas. 1971.*The Entropy Law and the Economic Process.* Harvard University Press.

Nicolas Georgescu-Roegen connected economic activity to entropy and physical consequences. His work was key in helping ecological economists understand the consequences of industrialism.

Prigogine, Ilya, and Isabelle Stengers. 1984.*Order out of Chaos: Man's New Dialogue with Nature.* Toronto; New York, NY: Bantam Books.

———. 1997.*The End of Certainty: Time, Chaos, and the New Laws of Nature.* New York: Free Press.

In *The End of Certainty,* Prigogine holds, "The more we know about our universe, the more difficult it becomes to believe in determinism." Determinism is based on a denial of the arrow of time. Irreversibility that occurs in complex, unstable systems such as radioactive decay, diffusion, weather, and life's emergence and evolution introduces the arrow of time and challenges determinism.

Prigogine notes in his Nobel prize lecture: "Since my adolescence, I have read many philosophical texts, and I still remember the spell *L'évolution créatrice* cast on me. More specifically, I felt that some essential message was embedded, still to be made explicit, in Bergson's remark: "The more deeply we study the nature of time, the better we understand that duration means invention, creation of forms, continuous elaboration of the absolutely new."

Wiener, Norbert. 1961.*Cybernetics or Control and Communication in the Animal and the Machine.*MIT Press.

Cybernetics is another particularly generative field. There are many definitions offered after Weiner. Louis Kauffman, President of the American Society for Cybernetics, states: "Cybernetics is the study of systems and processes that interact with themselves and produce themselves from themselves" Cybernetics, according to Gordon Pask, can be applied to information flows in all media from stars to brains.

"Schmidt Sting Pain Index." 2020. Wikipedia. December 6, 2020. https://en.wikipedia.org/wiki/Schmidt_sting_pain_index. Schmidt Pain Index.

5. Monetizing & Restoring Green Capital

Daniel, Kent D., Robert B. Litterman, and Gernot Wagner. 2019. "Declining CO2 Price Paths."*Proceedings of the National Academy of Sciences*116 (42): 20886–91. https://doi.org/10.1073/pnas.1817444116.

The $100 value for metric ton of carbon displacement in pro-
ceedings of the US National Academy of Science (NAS).

Klebnikov, Sergei. 2019. "Stopping Global Warming Will Cost $50
Trillion: Morgan Stanley Report." Forbes. October 24, 2019.
https://www.forbes.com/sites/sergeiklebnikov/2019/10/24/
stopping-global-warming-will-cost-50-trillion-morgan-stanley-
report/?sh=35d5e6fd51e2.

Sustainability Credits (SCs)

Morrison, Roy. 2020. "Climate Change and Inequality." Wall
Street International. November 1, 2020. https://wsimag.com/
economy-and-politics/63932-climate-change-and-inequality.

The advantage of accounting for SCs as capital on balance
sheets and as cash asset:

- SCs are easily measured by elimination of metric tons of carbon dioxide emissions by renewable energy systems.
- The value of SCs starting at $100 a ton per metric ton of
carbon emissions is based on estimates of consequences of
carbon emissions and dollar value of a putative carbon tax
to discourage carbon dioxide pollution.
- SCs, instead of a tax on carbon, are assets certified by investment banks, created by elimination of carbon dioxide pollution that is booked by those who undertake this activity.
- SCs represent the ability for future investment by financial
banking institutions in renewable energy (at the start).
- SCs are tradable instruments with real value that can be
turned into dollars/value through investment in new sustainability projects, as well as be sold forward and in a sec-
ondary market.
- SCs will represent and emerge as a store of value and a
measure of ecological conduct and ultimately as part of
the proper pursuit of the future ecological nature of fiduciary responsibility, which is essential for the future of free
markets.

- SCs are essentially a crucial transition step for allowing markets to aggressively and effectively pursue a successful, timely, and prompt resolution of the climate crisis.
- SCs represent an ecological tweaking of the accounting systems as opposed to a much more comprehensive transformation to value ecological consequences in all aspects of production, consumption, and investment.
- SCs, by simple changes in FASB and IASB rules and corresponding international accounting changes, will create a new ecological asset class and streams of value, encourage and reward investment in carbon dioxide elimination, and to do so in a matter that is focused on the key goal of carbon dioxide emissions elimination.

SCs can be managed by the Federal Financing Bank (FFB) and regulated by the Federal Reserve as they do any type of banking and financial asset or institution by adjusting interest rates, reserve requirements, purchasing SCs from increasing pollution levels resulting from too rapid development in an overheated economy or alternatively encourage more project development in a slowing economy.

The numbers are startling. The value of each year's operation of the $1.6 trillion investment in SCs (at $100 per metric ton of carbon dioxide displaced) is $.114 trillion. On the books of Green banks. But this can become $1 trillion in loans in year two.

However, this operation is not a one-time, one-year transaction. The existing systems keep adding $.114 trillion a year of SCs since they must keep operating to displace carbon dioxide. Thus, year four represents ten years of carbon displacement operation valued at $ 1.14 trillion.

It would be possible for developers, for example, to sell twenty-five years of Sustainability Credits forward to purchasers at a discounted NTP (Notice to Proceed). SC projects need to be approved by the BOC, but the ownership and use of SCs can spread throughout the banking system to help accelerate the renewable energy transformation and attain sustainability goals. SCs must be used as investment capital in new renewable or related systems, but as a store of value, they can be traded.

Blake, William. "Jerusalem." In *Milton: A Poem in Two Books.* Edmonton: London. 1886.

Jerusalem
And did those feet in ancient time
Walk upon Englands mountains green:
And was the holy Lamb of God,
On Englands pleasant pastures seen!

And did the Countenance Divine,
Shine forth upon our clouded hills?
And was Jerusalem builded here,
Among these dark Satanic Mills?

Bring me my Bow of burning gold:
Bring me my arrows of desire:
Bring me my Spear: O clouds unfold!
Bring me my Chariot of fire!

I will not cease from Mental Fight,
Nor shall my sword sleep in my hand:
Till we have built Jerusalem,
In Englands green & pleasant Land.

6. Justice, Always Justice

Rawls, John. 1975. *A Theory of Justice.* Cambridge, MA: Belknap Press.

7. Globalization of Sustainability

Skowron, Mal. 2019. "Why Efficiency Matters for Electric Cars." Green Energy Consumers Alliance. January 7, 2019. https://blog.greenenergyconsumers.org/blog/why-efficiency-matters-for-electric-cars.

FuelEconomy.gov. 2019. "How Can a Gallon of Gasoline Produce 20 Pounds of Carbon Dioxide?" FuelEconomy.Gov. 2019. https://www.fueleconomy.gov/feg/contentIncludes/co2_inc.htm.

8. Three Tons of Carbon Dioxide Per Person Per Year

Ritchie, Hannah. 2019. "Where in the World Do People Emit the Most CO2?" Our World in Data. October 4, 2019. https://ourworldindata.org/per-capita-co2.

Global Carbon Dioxide Emissions

Levin, Kelly, and Katie Lebling. 2019. "CO2 Emissions Climb to an All-Time High (Again) in 2019: 6 Takeaways from the Latest Climate Data." World Resources Institute. December 3, 2019. https://www.wri.org/blog/2019/12/co2-emissions-climb-all-time-high-again-2019-6-takeaways-latest-climate-data.

Clark, Duncan. 2011. "Which Nations Are Most Responsible for Climate Change?" The Guardian. April 21, 2011. http://www.theguardian.com/environment/2011/apr/21/countries-responsible-climate-change.

United Nations Department of Economic and Social Affairs (UNDESA). 2011. "The Clean Energy Technological Transformation." http://www.un.org/en/development/desa/policy/wess/wess_current/2011wess_chapter2.pdf.

9. Natural Gas: Part of the Problem, Not the Solution

Union of Concerned Scientists. 2014. "Infographic: The Climate Risks of Natural Gas." Union of Concerned Scientists. February 3, 2014. Https://www.UCSUSA.org/Resources/climate-risks-natural-gas.

10. Three Tons Per Person in National and Global Perspective

International Energy Agency (IEA). 2020. "Global CO2 Emissions in 2019 – Analysis." IEA. February 11, 2020. https://www.iea. org/articles/global-co2-emissions-in-2019.

EcoCivilization.info. n.d. "Three Tons Carbon Dioxide Per Person Per Year." EcoCivilization.Info. Accessed December 9, 2020. http://www.ecocivilization.info/three-tons-carbon-dioxide-per-person-per-year.html.

The good news is that there's a practical standard we can use to measure if we're living sustainably. It's simple. It's three tons of carbon dioxide emissions per person per year. At the average individual rate of three tons, yearly total global carbon dioxide emissions would be twenty-one gigatons for a population of seven billion.

As population rises, this number must decrease. And emissions must be combined with removal of carbon dioxide from the atmosphere into soil and biomass.

Hertwich, Edgar G., and Glen P. Peters. 2009. "Carbon Footprint of Nations: A Global, Trade-Linked Analysis."*Environmental Science & Technology*43 (16): 6414–20. https://doi.org/10.1021/es803496a.

11. Building an Ecological Civilization

Morrison, Roy. 1995.*Ecological Democracy*. Boston, MA: South End Press.

China International Working Groups. 2013. "Hangzhou Declaration." Ciwg.net. May 19, 2013. http://www.ciwg.net/hangzhou-declaration.html.

12. Global Perspectives and Ecological Glimmerings

Von Weizsäcker, Ernst Ulrich. 2009.*Factor Five: Transforming the Global Economy through 80% Improvements in Resource Productivity*. Sterling, VA: Earthscan/The Natural Edge Project.

Diamond, Jared M. 2011.*Collapse: How Societies Choose to Fail or Succeed.* New York: Penguin Books.

MacArthur, Ellen. "Towards the circular economy."*Journal of Industrial Ecology*2 (2013).
PDF available online: http://www3.weforum.org/docs/WEF_ENV_TowardsCircularEconomy_Report_2014.pdf

13. Two Basic Assumptions for a Green Republic

Gorz, André. 1979.*Ecology as Politics.* Boston: South End Press.
———. 1989.*Critique of Economic Reason.* London: Verso.

14. An Ecological Imperative

Morrison, Roy. 2007.*Markets, Democracy & Survival: How to Be Prosperous without Being Self-Destructive.* New Hampshire: Warner.

"One World." 1992. In*Development Dictionary: A Guide to Knowledge as Power.* Wolfgang Sachs.

Morrison, Roy. 1997.*We Build the Road as We Travel: Mondragon A Cooperative Social System.* Philadelphia, PA: New Society Publishers.

———. 2006.*Eco Civilization 2140: A 22nd Century History and Survivor's Journal.* Warner, NH: Writer's Pub. Cooperative.

Ostler, Jeffrey. 2020. "The Shameful Final Grievance of the Declaration of Independence." The Atlantic. February 8, 2020. https://www.theatlantic.com/ideas/archive/2020/02/americas-twofold-original-sin/606163/.
"The revolution wasn't only an effort to establish independence from the British—it was also a push to preserve slavery and suppress Native American resistance."

The Lehrman Institute. n.d. "The Founders and the Pursuit of Land." Lehrmaninstitute.org. https://lehrmaninstitute.org/history/founders-land.html.
Washington and Jefferson and westward expansion

15. Prices as Ecological Tools

Asian Development Bank. 2011. "Guangdong Energy Efficiency and Environment Improvement Investment Program – Tranche 3." Asian Development Bank. September 5, 2011. https://www.adb.org/projects/39653-043/main.

International Labour Organization, *The Double Dividend And Environmental Tax Reforms In The European Union.* Online: http://www.ilo.org/public/english/bureau/inst/research/ecinst/dp13.pdf.

Yan, Xu. 2011. "China's VAT Experience."*Taxhistory.org.* Tax Analysts. http://www.taxhistory.org/www/freefiles.nsf/Files/YAN-25.pdf/$file/YAN-25.pdf.

World Bank (2010). "Lessons from the Implementation of the Republic of Korea's Green Stimulus". World Bank: Infrastructure Recovery and Assets (IFRA) Platform. June 2010. http://siteresources.world-bank.org/INTSDNET/Resources/5944695-1247775731647/INFRA_Korea_Newsletter.pdf

16. Alternative Regimes for Quick Response

Stanway, David. 2019. "China CO2 Emissions to Peak in 2022, Ahead of Schedule: Government Researcher."*Reuters,* September 5, 2019. https://www.reuters.com/article/idUSL3N25W195.

Fu Peng, 2014. "China approves plan to combat climate change." Xinhua. On line: http://news.xinhuanet.com/english/sci/2014-09/19/c_133655788.htm.

Faulkner, Roger, Roy Morrison, and Jennifer Wells. 2013. "A China-East Asia Efficient Renewable Supergrid."*China International Working Groups.* China International Working Groups. http://www.ciwg.net/files/74235701.pdf.

Statista. 2020. "Carbon Dioxide Emissions from Energy Consumption in the U.S. from 1975 to 2020." Statista. Statista. 2020. https://www.statista.com/statistics/183943/us-carbon-dioxide-emissions-from-1999/.

Carbon dioxide emissions totals

Kyu-won Jeong, Kwang-hee Hong, Sung-yun Hong, Kab-ho Park, Hong-gyun Kim, Bong-soo Moon, 2014.1 Construction the North-East Asian Supergrid for Co-prosperity and Peace. Cigre. Online: http://www.cigre-thailand.org/tncf/events/aorc2014/ full_paper/1076R.pdf.

Asian Development Bank. 2008. "MFF: Guangdong Energy Efficiency and Environment Improvement Investment Program – Tranche 1." Asian Development Bank. June 9, 2008. https://www.adb.org/ projects/39653-023/main#project-pds.

17. Justice, Justice: Back to Justice

Brundtland Commission. 1987.*Our Common Future*. Edited by Volker Hauff. Suffolk, EN: Oxford University Press.

The 1987 definition of sustainable development as meeting present needs without compromising future generations was hardly a clarion call for change. Less well known is the following injunction that "sustainable development requires that those who are affluent adopt life styles within the planet's ecological means—in their use of energy, for example." And that is followed by the conclusion, "Yet in the end sustainable development is not a fixed state of harmony, but a process of change …" (Brundtland, page 28, par. 29 and 30)

Morrison, Roy. 2007."Part VI: A New Golden Rule: Crafting Ethics and Values for an Ecological Democracy." In *A Renewable Energy World and Other Adventures in Sustainability*. RockItScience Productions, LLC. https://studylib.net/doc/7708763.

Curry, Patrick. 2006. *Ecological Ethics: An Introduction*. London: Polity Press.

18. Inequality as Reality

Marx, Karl. 1939.*Grundrisse: Foundations of the Critique of Political Economy (Rough Draft)*. Translated by Martin Nicolaus. Penguin

Books. https://www.marxists.org/archive/marx/works/1857/grundrisse/index.htm.

Rothwell, Jonathan. 2020. "The Effects of COVID-19 on International Labor Markets: An Update." Brookings. May 27, 2020. https://www.brookings.edu/research/the-effects-of-covid-19-on-international-labor-markets-an-update/.

19. Investments in Sustainability

Weaver, John. 2020. "Solar Industry Gets $27.8 Billion in Corporate Finance for Company Building and Projects in 2019." PV Magazine. January 10, 2020. https://pv-magazine-usa.com/2020/01/10/solar-power-gets-27-8-billion-in-corporate-finance-for-new-companies-and-projects-in-2019/.

20. Markets from Both Sides

Smith, Adam. (1776) 2000. *The Wealth of Nations*. New York: Random House International.

"Miami-Dade County Poverty Statistics." n.d. LiveStories. https://www.livestories.com/statistics/florida/miami-dade-county-poverty.

21. Green Republic as a Complex System

Ulanowicz, Robert E. 2010. *Ecology: The Ascendant Perspective*. New York: Columbia University Press.

Margulis, Lynn. 1998. *Symbiotic Planet: A New Look at Evolution*. New York: Basic Books.

Eldredge, Niles, and Gould, S. J. 1972 (1985). "Punctuated Equilibria: An Alternative to Phyletic Gradualism." In T.J.M. Schopf, ed., *Models in Paleobiology*. San Francisco: Freeman Cooper. pp. 82-115. Reprinted in N. Eldredge *Time Frames*. Princeton: Princeton Univ. Press.

22. Ecosystems and Being

Hunt-Badiner, Allan. 1990. "The Perceptual Implications of Gaia." In *Dharma Gaia: A Harvest of Essays in Buddhism and Ecology.* Berkeley, Calif.: Parallax Press.

Laughlin, Robert B. 2006. *A Different Universe: Reinventing Physics from the Bottom Down.* New York: Basic Books.

See the work of Stuart Kauffman for discussion of life and self-organization and with discussions of implications for social and economic forms including:

Kauffman, Stuart A. 1996. *At Home in the Universe: The Search for Laws of Self-Organization and Complexity.* New York: Oxford University Press.

———. 1993. *The Origins of Order: Self-Organization and Selection in Evolution.* New York: Oxford University Press.

———. 2000. *Investigations.* New York: Oxford University Press.

———. 2010. *Reinventing the Sacred: A New View of Science, Reason, and Religion.* Basic Books.

For discussion of Kauffman's work see:

www.iscid.org/stuartkauffman-chat.php

See "Which Way Now" *New Scientist,* May 3, 2008 for a discussion of competing theories of everything including:

- Causal Dynamical Triangulation approach to quantum gravity.
http://www.phys.uu.nl/~loll/Web/press/newscientist.pdf

Quantum mechanics and general relativity have been the mathematically incompatible manifestations of the four basic forces of nature—gravity, electromagnetism, the strong force holding atoms together, and the weak force of radioactive decay.

Quantum gravity given the approach of Ambjørn, Jurkiewicz, and Loll offers a common solution to the behavior of the very small and the very large, one in which space-time as we know it is an emergent feature and where time runs in one direction only. Time machines will have to remain in the domain of science fiction.

For a semi-popular article (with equations) on an emergent self-organizing universe by the theoretical physicists see:

> Ambjørn, J., Jurkiewicz, J., and Loll, R. Mar. 31, 2008. "The Self-Organized de Sitter Universe." http://www.phys.uu.nl/~loll/Web/press/desitteressay.pdf
>
> "Here is what we can do in 2008: a quantum ensemble of essentially structureless, microscopic constituents, which interact according to simple local rules dictated by gravity, causality and quantum theory, can produce a 'quantum universe,' which on large scales matches perfectly a classical, four-dimensional de Sitter universe! The derivation of this unprecedented result, obtained in the context of a candidate theory for quantum gravity based on Causal Dynamical Triangulations, is remarkable for a number of reasons."

Ambjorn, Jan, Jerzy Jurkiewicz, and Renate Loll. 2008. "The Self-Organizing Quantum Universe." *Scientific American.* July 2008. P. 42-49.

23. Making Article One Explicit

Morrison, Roy. n.d. "Global Ecological Economic Growth." EcoCivilization.Info. http://www.ecocivilization.info/global-ecological-economic-growth.html.

Greene, Herman. 2016. "Transition to An Ecological Civilization." Center for Ecozoic Studies. Sept. 25, 2016. http://www.ecozoicsocieties.org/musings/2016/wealth-demographics-transition-ecological-civilization/

24. Property in the Green Republic

George, Henry. (1879) 2006.*Progress and Poverty*. The Robert Schalkenbach Foundation. http://www.henrygeorge.org/pcontents.htm.

Elinor, Ostrom 1990. *Governing the Commons: The Evolution of Institutions for Collective Action*. Cambridge, UK: Cambridge University Press.

25. Technological Questions

Sundance Solar, 2015. Sunbender Do-it-Yourself Solar LED Jar Light Kit – Pre-wired, no soldering. http://store.sundancesolar.com/sunbender-do-it-yourself-solar-led-jar-light-kit-pre-wired-no-soldering/.
This system is being adapted for Namibian student assembly and sale.

Morrison, Roy 2012. "Building an Efficient Renewable Energy System: Advanced Energy performance Contracting as Key Tool." http://www.ecocivilizationweebly.com/competitively-bid-feed-in-tariff.html.

Czisch, Gregor. 2011.*Scenarios for a Future Electricity Supply: Cost-Optimised Variations on Supplying Europe and Its Neighbours with Electricity from Renewable Energies*. London: Institution of Engineering and Technology.

Hardt, Marah, and Carl Safina. 2008. "Covering Ocean Acidification: Chemistry and Considerations." Yale Climate Connections. June 24, 2008. https://yaleclimateconnections.org/2008/06/covering-ocean-acidification-chemistry-and-considerations/.

26. Green Republic: Athens not Sparta

Norgaard, Richard B. 2010. "A Coevolutionary Interpretation of Ecological Civilization." New Economics Institute. http://new-economicsinstitute.org/webfm_send/23.

Shengxian, Zhou. 2011. "Promote Green Development, Uplift Ecological Civilization." *China, Economy, Green Energy.* http://neurope.eu/greenchina/articles/promote-green-development-uplift-ecological-civilization-2011.

Jenkins, T. N. 2002. "Chinese Traditional Culture: The Marriage of Ecological Wisdom and Science." *Ecological Economics.* Volume 40, Issue 1, January 2002, pp. 39-52.

27. Supporting Ecological Ends

Tiwald, Justin, and Bryan W. Van Norden, eds. 2014.*Readings in Later Chinese Philosophy.* Indianapolis: Hackett Publishing Company, Inc.

Hamilton, Alexander, James Madison, and John Jay. (1901). Smith, Goldwin (ed.) *The Federalist.* New York: The Colonial Press. The Federalist Papers written in 1787-1788.

de Tocqueville, Alexis. 1835. Vol. 2 Part 2, Chapter 2, "Individualism in Democratic Countries." In *Democracy in America.* Henry Reeve translation, revised and corrected, 1899. http://xroads.virginia. edu/~hyper/DETOC/ch2_02.htm

"Individualism is a novel expression, to which a novel idea has given birth. Our fathers were only acquainted with egoism (selfishness). Selfishness is a passionate and exaggerated love of self, which leads a man to connect everything with himself and to prefer himself to everything in the world. Individualism is a mature and calm feeling, which disposes each member of the community to sever himself from the mass of his fellows and to draw apart with his family and his friends, so that after he has thus formed a little circle of his own, he willingly leaves society at large to itself... individualism, at first, only saps the virtues of public life; but in the long run it attacks and destroys all others and is at length absorbed in downright selfishness...

As social conditions become more equal, the number of persons increases who, although they are neither rich nor powerful enough to exercise any great influence over their fellows, have nevertheless acquired or retained sufficient education and fortune to satisfy their own wants. They owe nothing to any man, they expect nothing from any man; they acquire the habit of always considering themselves as standing alone, and they are apt to imagine that their whole destiny is in their own hands.

Thus not only does democracy make every man forget his ancestors, but it hides his descendants and separates his contemporaries from him; it throws him back forever upon himself alone and threatens in the end to confine him entirely within the solitude of his own heart."

28. Tools for Ecological and Social Justice

Van Parijs, Phillipe, and Yannick Vanderborght. 2017.*Basic Income: A Radical Proposal for a Free Society and a Sane Economy.*Cambridge: Harvard University Press.

World Trade Organization. n.d. "The Environment: A Specific Concern." World Trade Organization. https://www.wto.org/ english/thewto_e/whatis_e/tif_e/bey2_e.htm.

29. Sustainability and the Social

Lovelock, James. 1995.*The Ages of Gaia: A Biography of Our Living Earth.* New York: W.W. Norton.

Hansen, Eric, Rajat Panwar, and Richard P. Vlosky. 2014.*The Global Forest Sector: Changes, Practices, and Prospects.* Boca Raton, FL: Taylor & Francis.

McGill University. 2011. "Feeding the World While Protecting the Planet." Channels: McGill University and Events. McGill. October 12, 2011. https://www.mcgill.ca/channels/news/ feeding-world-while-protecting-planet-202006.

Brugère, Cécile, and Neil Ridler. 2004.*Global Aquaculture Outlook in the Next Decades: An Analysis of National Aquaculture Production*

Forecasts to 2030. Food and Agriculture Organization of the United Nations.

30. Industrial Business to Ecological Business as Usual

Morrison, Roy. n.d. "The BIG (Basic Income Grant) and the BEE (Basic Energy Entitlement): A Sustainable Convergence." EcoCivilization.Info. https://www.ecocivilization.info/a-big-and-a-bee.html.

Oppenheim, Jerrold and Theo MacGregor. 2008. *Energy Efficiency Equals Economic Development*. Energy Corp.

Hewes, Will. 2008. *Creating Jobs and Stimulating the Economy through Investment in Green Water Infrastructure*. American Rivers, Inc. http://www.americanrivers.org/assets/pdfs/green-infrastructure-docs/green_infrastructure_stimulus_white_paper_final.pdf

The National Association of Regulatory Utility Commissioners. 2007. *Decoupling for Electric & Gas Utilities: Frequently Asked Questions (FAQ)*. http://www.epa.gov/statelocalclimate/documents/pdf/supp_mat_decoupling_elec_gas_utilities.pdf.

31. Electric Grid

Lovins, Amory. 1989. "The Negawatt Revolution: Solving the CO2 Problem." In-person Keynote presented at the Green Energy Conference. http://www.ccnr.org/amory.html.

Morrison, Roy. 2008. "Rising Sun for Electric Cars | Carnegie Council for Ethics in International Affairs." Carnegie Council for Ethics in International Affairs. April 22, 2008. https://www.carnegiecouncil.org/publications/archive/policy_innovations/innovations/000039.

Morrison, Roy, and Pentti Aalto. 2008. "Cogeneration Can Slash Carbon and Costs." Carnegie Council for Ethics in International

Affairs. August 14, 2008. https://www.carnegiecouncil.org/publications/archive/policy_innovations/innovations/000069.

32. Technical Complexity and Technological Evolution

Anderlini, Jamil. 2007. "Sold Down the River: Environmental Hubris Exacts a Heavy Price on the Yangtze."*Financial Times*, November 1, 2007.

This explores a classic case of a nation-state in action in support of the Three Gorges dam in China, the world's largest construction project. After the Tiananmen Square, the Chinese state stopped effective opposition to the project. Now in operation, the dam has resulted in some predicted and some surprising consequences. Changing Yangtze water flows has led to the expected relocation of 1.3 million people and the growth of massive silt deposits that are choking the river, threatening the dam's operation. But unexpected was the growth of toxic algae blooms from lowered water flow and agricultural, municipal, and industrial pollution; collapsing new river banks; and tidal salt water penetrating farther up the Shanghai costal estuaries.

33. Ecological Automation: Driverless Cars

Green, Hank. 2007. "The 'Green' Toyota Backlash is ON!" EcoGeek. http://www.ecogeek.org/content/view/1051/.

In 2007, even Toyota, hybrid car king, is opposing increases in US car mileage CAFE standards to levels that would be impact sales of its profitable Tundra monster pick-up truck. This is industrialism in action and a very poor application of autonomy and self-governance.

The exercise of freedom and democracy and an ecological ethics means social decisions as well as economic and ethical personal choices to drive less or buy a car that gets higher gas mileage.

Brazil, for example, by producing huge amounts of cane ethanol, for which its land and climate is well suited, can reduce
the climate impact of driving flex-fueled cars by 80 percent or
more. Carbon, of course, is not the only ecological problem of
the personal automobile. But mitigating the carbon problem
is a good start. A comparable US alternative is not using corn
ethanol (currently only 20 percent climate neutral), but using
plug-in hybrids served by an increasingly renewably powered
electric grid, driving lightweight, carbon fiber hyper cars, and
using cellulosic ethanol.

34. Global Forms

Wallerstein, Immanuel. 2007.*World Systems Analysis: An Introduction.*
Durham, North Carolina: Duke University Press.
Bookchin, Murray. (1982) 2005.*The Ecology of Freedom: The
Emergence and Dissolution of Hierarchy.* Edinburgh: AK Press.
Sustainability, in response to necessity, will establish overtime the
lineaments of an emerging peace system organized around
democratic continental unions of nations. Historically, democ-
racies never, or almost never, resort to war with one another.
See:
Weart, Spencer R. 2000. *Never at War: Why Democracies Will Not Fight
One Another.* New Haven: Yale University Press.
The pursuit of sustainability in the democratic context will
alleviate the underlying causes of belligerency and encourage political instead of military responses to disputes that are
the province of democratic systems in their dealings with one
another.

www.ingramcontent.com/pod-product-compliance
Lightning Source LLC
Chambersburg PA
CBHW072131270326
41931CB00010B/1729